Thoughts for Jesse

A Father's Tribute

NATHAN STRONG

ISBN: 1439268487
ISBN-13: 9781439268483

Cover photo by Heather Strong

For my son, Jesse, who asked me to write this book for him. Jesse was truly blessed to have found something to live for and something worth dying for. He gave his life for his country, for the Iraqi people, for you, for me, on January 26, 2005, in Haqlanya, Iraq.

Notes to himself in the front of Jesse's Bible

Mentality to have as the Lord
makes you a perfect man.

Definition: "One who has a clear sense of
self in relation to the Lord." In other words
"Being willing to be completely honest with
yourself and with the Lord, unafraid of what
you might find out or what the Lord might
point out about you." – Ephesians 4

The means –1 John 1:5-7

Remember: God is the One Who brings about the
changes – all we have to do is see the
problem, be honest about it, and tell the
Lord to take care of it. Ask the Lord to
shine His light in every area, and say "I am
willing to deal with it", and He will!

(Green Letters)

Ask A Mountain, "Why?"

To ask God, "Why?'
     is like asking a mountain, "Why?"

With all its majesty
     and grandeur
     and inscrutability,
Who could ever
     understand the answer,
     anyway?

With words from your heart
     like "Awesome!" and "Cool!"
You have to go
     with what you know,
And leave the rest,
     as He knows best.

It's worth it
     just to see the mountain.

I have enclosed this copy of the original list of topics that Jesse wanted me to address as an indication of the kinds of things he was interested in, as well as the things that we would have talked about over the years. – NWS

Jesse Strong – Age 23   Summer 2004

Dad's Random Theology Topics

1. The purpose of life (include aspect of God interfacing)
2. Marriage (and growth as a married couple)
3. Divorce
4. Remarriage
5. Purpose of the church (include definition of the church as opposed to Israel + the Gentiles)
6. Prayer - purpose of, approach to, methods
7. Pastoring - purpose, authority, responsibility
8. Gospel / Salvation - work of the HS, approach, delivery
9. Parenting - raising, teaching children, family (aspects)
10. Hermeneutics - system of
11. Counseling - methods / philosophy, pastoral, marriage
12. Logic - use of reason, system of thought
13. Ethics - approach: greater good or lesser of 2 evils?, lying
14. Discipleship - importance, methods
15. Revival - church, cultural, etc. - philosophy of
16. Theology - approach to the study of God
17. Apologetics + Evangelism - cultural outreach strategies
18. Missions - philosophy of
19. Decision making - & the will of God
20. Homiletics - sermon prep, delivery, teaching styles
21. Pastoral care - visiting, dealing w/ tragedies, etc.
22. "Ministry" - definition, meaning

TABLE OF CONTENTS

PREFACE: An introduction to Jesse   **ix**

INTRODUCTION   **xvii**
CHAPTER ONE: The Purpose of Life   **1**
The genius of creation... the beginning of wisdom... the purpose of life... and live happily ever after... why is the world a mess?... sharing the consequences... life is too short... life is not fair – for whom?... the puzzle of life... the mystery of life... dad's philosophy of life... the overview of history... the Garden of Eden revisited... a matter of focus...
CHAPTER TWO: Marriage   **25**
Some basic concepts for marriage... love redefined... love fulfills life, marriage, and the law... a few collected words of wisdom for marriage... love and the gifts of the Spirit
CHAPTER THREE: Divorce and Remarriage   **35**
CHAPTER FOUR: The Purpose of the Church   **39**
Is the church Israel?... basic blueprint for the church... game plan for the church
CHAPTER FIVE: The Secret of Prayer   **47**
CHAPTER SIX:
Pastoring: Purpose, Authority, Responsibility   **67**
CHAPTER SEVEN:
Gospel/ Salvation, Apologetics and Evangelism   **73**
Getting to know God... God introduces Himself to us... obtaining mercy and finding grace... reconciliation... the postmodern era... approach and delivery... one important key
CHAPTER EIGHT: Parenting   **91**
CHAPTER NINE: Hermeneutics   **107**
Basic rules... cautionary rules
CHAPTER TEN: Counseling   **115**
Introduction... basic ideas... pastoral counseling... marriage counseling
CHAPTER ELEVEN: Logic   **123**
Introduction... use of reason... system of thought... breaking out of Jonah thinking
CHAPTER TWELVE: Ethics   **129**

CHAPTER THIRTEEN: Discipleship   **135**
CHAPTER FOURTEEN: Revival   **141**
CHAPTER FIFTEEN: Theology   **143**
> *Reflections of God... glimpses of God... the ultimate Reflection... the offer of personal experience... applied theology*

CHAPTER SIXTEEN: Missions   **157**
> *The call to missions... a personal example... message for the world*

CHAPTER SEVENTEEN:
Decision Making and the Will of God   **163**
> *Introduction... God's will for beginners... God's will for His older children... Dad's long term plan for having the mind of Christ... the advantage of doing God's will... legacies... plans A, B and C for life... our job... free will – freedom within the fence... blockages... the source of discontentment... I surrender all – now what?... one last thought*

CHAPTER EIGHTEEN: Homiletics   **179**
> *Introduction... sermon preparation... some secrets to decent preaching... sermon delivery... teaching styles*

CHAPTER NINETEEN: Ministry   **191**
> *Definition... the right attitude... the right ministry... the right purpose*

BONUS FEATURE: A Shepherd's Story   **201**
APPENDIX: "New Normal"   **211**

Preface

An introduction to Jesse:

The eulogy at his memorial service, February 4, 2005,
at which Rev. Jerry Falwell officiated

*Written by his brother Matthew
and his sister Heather*

JESSE WARNER STRONG LIVED AN amazing life in just
24 years. Jesse's life was so vibrant and touched so many
people, it makes it difficult to sum up the impact he had
on the world around him. In fact, Jesse's life was so full
and rich that we cannot possibly cover it all here or in
the slideshow which we will see later. Jesse's life is best
embodied by this Bible verse, "I thank God upon every
remembrance of you." He left us with such a storehouse
of joyful memories that they will last us a lifetime. That
was his greatest gift to us.

Even as an infant, Jesse was always smiling. As a
baby, no one could make him smile and laugh as easily
as his older brother, Matthew. This bond of laughter
would continue throughout his life and whether they
were sitting next to each other in church, working

together for the summer, or any time they were in each other's company, whatever Matthew did would always make Jesse laugh. The same was true for his father, Nate. While Vicki and Heather would roll their eyes at Nate's antics, Jesse would always burst out laughing. When Jesse left his job at Ray's Market to start his education at Liberty University, his co-workers awarded him with a plaque bearing the title, "Happiest Man Alive" in honor of his constant smile and laughter.

But Jesse didn't even need people around him to make him laugh. He was able to amuse himself regardless of where he was. When walking through the grocery store, one of his favorite things to do was to pretend to run into poles, or to run into signs on the sidewalk, just because he thought the shocked expressions on people's faces were hilarious. As he was walking off the platform at his college graduation he pretended to trip and stumble, knocking his cap sideways on his head. Jesse was extremely proud of himself for this and the memory of it never failed to make him laugh.

During his time in Vermont, Jesse was very active in the local community. He helped with a weekly after-school club at the Albany Elementary school, and mentored a young boy there for a year. Every year he helped with Vacation Bible School and always praised the children warmly for their little accomplishments throughout the day. He especially loved to call the small boys "big guy", and their little chests would swell with pride. For Jesse, ministry was a way of life. Whether he was playing whiffle ball with the kids after church, or helping them climb trees on the church property, he continually invested in the lives of those around him.

The way he treated others naturally built them up. Jesse became extremely close with one family in particular, acting as a big brother and friend to the three children. Even while Jesse spent the majority of the year at college, when he was home he always made a point to stop by their house just to spend time with them and play with them. He was so proud as he watched them get older and often commented, "They're so much cooler than I was at their age!"

Jesse had a multitude of interests and pursued each one with enthusiasm and focus. Besides his amazing carving talents, baseball and wiffleball took up the majority of his free time as a child and teen. In fact, Jesse couldn't sit still during his studies for more than half an hour before taking a break to go swing his bat for a while. Jesse had natural talent for the game and with his intense passion to do his best and great teamwork attitude he was called the "secret weapon" on his Pee-Wee team. He loved all the guys he played with on the Craftsbury teams he was a part of. He really enjoyed playing for UCA and his greatest moment was being able to play on Centennial Field for the state championship, but even more amazing was the graciousness with which he handled the loss.

During his high school years he also excelled at bow hunting and bowling. He went so far as to tape professional bowling on TV so he could study professional level technique in order to improve his own game (he bowled a high game of 265 and was the highest scoring bowler in his league at Liberty University). Later he turned his attention to golf and studied Tiger Woods in the same way, always practicing and improving. He transferred his habit of having his wiffle bat with him at all times to his golf club, even taking it with him on Heather's college tours and family trips. In the winter he would hit golf balls into the field behind the house, then run out to find them in the snow. And it was this same perfectionism that earned him a marksmanship score of 241 out of a possible 250 at boot camp. The course record at Parris Island, South Carolina (out of all the recruits that have passed through its gates) is 245.

He was competitive, but was extremely competitive with himself. He always felt that he could do something better or could improve one of his skills. To accomplish this, he made a practice of doing things the hard way. When he went to Liberty as a freshman, he insisted that he fly there by himself rather than having his family drive him down. He was eager to become a man and saw the trip alone as a step towards achieving that. Jesse soaked up the academics at college, where he turned his perfectionism from sports to classes. He became an extremely dedicated student, but by junior year he had loosened up and made plenty of time to goof off with the guys in dorm 9.

As one of the Spiritual Life Directors on the hall, he invested in the young men around him, leading Bible Studies and prayer groups, staying up late to cut their hair, or hanging out in their rooms. Jesse was a friend to everyone. No one was beneath his notice. The next year he became a Resident Assistant with his co-SLD,

Nate. The two of them had a lasting impact on every young man on their hall. Yet again, Jesse never stopped befriending those who needed a friend most, and we have received letters and cards from parents whose son's lives will be forever altered because of his friendship, spiritual guidance and example of good fashion.

His desire to grow as a person and as a man is also why he joined the Marines. He felt it a duty to serve his country and he wanted nothing less than the toughest challenge, knowing the Marines' reputation for having the hardest boot camp, except for Special Forces. His family worried that the Marines would take away his carefree humor and goofiness, but that couldn't have been farther from the truth. It took a half hour of a patient photographer's time to get the picture of Jesse with a straight face, which has now filled our TV screens and newspaper pages. And his Drill Instructors only gave Jesse more people to imitate when he got home.

Yet he and his family were incredibly proud of his service in the Marine Corps, and this was not an association that he took lightly. He loved their combination of principles and precision. When 9/11 happened just weeks after his graduation from boot camp he told his concerned mother, "Mom, I'm ready to go if they need me". He wore his uniform proudly whenever he could, sometimes even when formal attire was not required or expected. He even purchased a uniform for a close family friend, Lee Harvey, who was a Korean War Vet, so they could march together in the Memorial Day Parade. He was always taking his Marine workbooks with him in case he had some time to study. It was this enthusiasm and commitment to the service of his country that earned him the promotion to Sergeant on January 1st, after just 3 and a half years, a virtually unheard-of achievement for a Reservist. He was also the only Marine to have hand sanitizer with him at all times during his weekend drills.

Eight months after graduating from Liberty, Jesse began studying theology and apologetics at Southern Evangelical Theological Seminary. His decision to go to that particular school was almost entirely based on the reputation of the school's president, Norman Geisler, one of the most knowledgeable Christian thinkers and scholars of our time. Again, Jesse's desire to do the best he could spilled over into his personal walk with Jesus. He went to seminary for only 2 reasons, to know more about Jesus and to be able to answer questions from those within his ever widening circle of influence. The semester he spent at seminary was very gratifying for Jesse, and he was sure that God used that time to prepare him for sharing his faith with his buddies in Iraq. In situations such as combat, even the bravest man will have questions about God, and Jesse used his knowledge every day, and was the honorary Chaplain of his unit for a time.

His amazing attitude and character proved invaluable in Iraq. He always volunteered for the tough jobs that few wanted to do, including the mission on January 26th, 2005. He entertained all those around him with his dancing, smile, jokes, and sincere desire to know how everyone was doing. He received tons of packages and always shared with those around him. He even entertained his family and friends at home with his humorous letters, while still sharing his strong faith and wisdom beyond his years. His last postcard came on Wednesday, one week after his ultimate sacrifice in Iraq. He had drawn another funny picture of himself and in his message he said "I'm excited for what the future holds!" How right he was to be excited. The birth of a democracy he died to help establish, and his eternity at the right hand of God. It just doesn't get any more exciting than that.

Jesse never formulated a clear career path, and he often joked about being excited for the future as long as it didn't involve work, or about asking his Mom to come up with a career for him. However, his true career goal, from a young age, was to be the man God wanted him to be. That was always his main focus, and the motivation for his drive to learn more about God. While at Liberty, he and his roommate, Nate, would talk for hours about theology and the Bible. Nearly every time he called home he would have a question for his father on some verse or doctrinal issue. After each class in seminary, Jesse would never fail to ask his teacher, Dr. Geisler, several questions on the lecture that day. His recent years were devoted almost solely to knowing God better, and God honored that by calling Jesse to meet Him in person. What an amazing privilege!

Jesse's father, mother, sister, and brother especially wish to express the peace and joy they are experiencing by saying, "There can be no question that this is the presence of God and the prayers of thousands surrounding us. Had we tried to foresee this situation, it is doubtful that anyone would have predicted that we would be constantly praising God, in the midst of our sorrow, for the Lord's peace that passes all understanding and for the hope of meeting Jesse again in our eternal heavenly home. Not only do we feel the presence of our Lord, but also the presence of Jesse as he experiences the ultimate joy of being with our Savior. We are daily uplifted by the Prince of Peace, and are continually seeing the ways that God is glorified through Jesse's death. We are also constantly reminded of God's unfailing mercy towards us.

"Our Father knew from the beginning that this would be Jesse's time, yet He wanted to make it as easy for us as possible. From Matthew, Jesse, and Heather being home-schooled so we spent as much time together as a family as we could, to God's grace in bringing Matthew and Heather together in Pittsburgh hours before receiving the news of Jesse's death, to a million other tiny mercies that become evident each day, we see the loving hand of God always with us. We know no greater joy than that Jesse gave his life proudly and bravely for his country, and that through his life and death Christ has been glorified, and through His mercy we have no regrets concerning our lives together with Jesse. It is our privilege to be used by God for His purpose, and through His grace we are truly able to exclaim, 'Praise the Lord, it is well with my soul!'"

Introduction

"Dad always does things differently..."

JESSE WAS IN SEMINARY, LEARNING how to help people with their faith. He was studying systematic theology. Theology was our favorite topic of discussion wherever we were or whatever we were doing, so it was only natural that he would come up with the idea of having me write some of it down for him. He said I was the only person he knew who had only studied the Bible, unaffected by any other book of theology. He wanted me to write down the ideas we had shared, so he could enjoy them through the years when I wasn't there.

When I told him I couldn't write a systematic theology book, because it was against my convictions, he wanted to know why. I told him the Bible was not systematic, most likely for a reason, perhaps because, by its very nature, life is pretty random. Far be it from me to think I could straighten it out. Random theology would be the best I could do. In fact, even better, if he would write a list of questions he wanted me to answer; I would try to address them. So, in the summer before he left for Iraq, he sent me the list which I have enclosed at the beginning of this book.

He had told me that I could write the book for him after I finished the novel I was working on, but when he was killed in action in January, it helped me through the initial stages of grief to begin to write for him. About a year later, I was strong enough to go back to my novel. When that was finished, I returned to this book, but the momentum was gone. I couldn't see what the point was, if he was never going to get to read it. He was the only reason I had even begun it. There were already plenty of theology books.

It's been two years, and people keep asking about the book. Jesse's impact continues, and people are interested in what interested him. And then there's the promise I made to a young mother who called when she heard of his death. She had read about Jesse, was impressed with his life and wondered if I had any parenting tips. I told her she would have to wait for the book, as that was one of the questions Jesse wanted me to address. The pressure of this unfinished business has begun to rekindle the momentum, although the reason has changed.

And so, I'm at it again, doing it for Jesse. It's no longer a theology book, however, since he won't be reading it. Now it's simply a collection of thoughts for Jesse which will, I hope, honor his memory and further his ministry of helping people with their faith. Rather than being formal, highly technical or exhaustive, it is written in the manner of a father sharing with his son something from the heart, something that would help him with his life and with his growth in a relationship with Jesus, the most wonderful Person in the universe to know.

You will find some important theological points here, many of which are seminal thoughts, designed to stimulate your own thinking and exploration, rather than being an exhaustive explanation. You will find some of my observations about life, relationships and ministry based on thirty-five years of Bible study and application about which Jesse always questioned me and which always seemed to fascinate him. And you will also find interesting trivia and what I call gems of thought scattered throughout, as they were sprinkled all through our conversations, as they are through life, just to make things interesting. I am writing, not as an expert, but as a fascinated participant and studious observer.

Accompanying the theological points you may find scripture references at the end of the section for further study. With all the rest, you will find scripture references if they come to mind at the time. If there are none, these sections are offered in the spirit of Paul's honesty, integrity and experience, as expressed in the seventh chapter of first Corinthians, verses 12, 25 and 40.

Jesse still encourages me, as he always did. Recently I went bowling with our men's group, just for fun. I wasn't paying much attention during the first game and wound up with the lowest score in the group. In the second game I began to hear Jesse's voice. Not to me, but to himself, as I had heard it so many times when we bowled together in our local men's league. I heard him saying to himself, "Settle down. Focus. Hit your mark. Get your form right, and the score will take care of itself."

I began to do just that, letting Jesse's passion to do better wash over me. I began to settle down and pay attention. I focused on good form, and I began to hit my mark more consistently. I began to "make the good adjustment", one of his favorite sayings. Through that game and the next I listened to Jesse's self-coaching, and the score did take care of itself. I wound up with the highest score in the group and was accused of hustling them, but it was just Jesse's good influence, the effect he had on all those around him.

Jesse always stimulated me to do more, to do better, and he still has that effect on me. That's really the reason for this book. I hope it has a little of that effect on you.

Chapter one

The Purpose of Life

The genius of creation

IN HIS INCREDIBLE WISDOM, GOD created a system in which anyone, anywhere, no matter what their circumstances, has the potential for happiness. This is possible because true joy comes from a vital relationship with Him, independent of the situation. It is not dependent upon wealth, status, location or anything we ordinarily think is necessary for happiness. Consider these best and worst case scenarios as examples.

Let's begin with a worst case scenario. I was in my teens during the Vietnam War. My best friend's brother was killed in that war. I lived with the daily realization that there were American servicemen lost to the world in jungle prison camps over there, perhaps still are. This weighed heavily on my heart, and I prayed for them often. I finally realized that God was not limited by the situation. He could bless and encourage them and give them joy, purpose and fulfillment in a Viet Cong prison camp as well as He could anyone in much better circumstances, as they testified when they came home. That drastic image was one of the things that helped me understand this whole concept, which applies to any situation which we would ordinarily think of as being extremely negative, thanks to God's creative genius.

For a best case scenario, consider my life. I've had my share of hard times and heartaches, but on my worst day I have had so much to be thankful for and to be happy about. On my worst days, I woke up beside a wonderful, loving wife. I was greeted by three children who were the delight of my life. Though never rich, I have always had enough to eat and to keep up with the bills sooner or later. And besides all that, which is more than enough for anyone, I have known the gracious presence of the Lord, Who is my joy, my strength, my help and my constant Friend.

What more could I ask? And that's on my worst day! Think about how awesome my good days have been.

References: - true joy: Ps.16:11, Is.61:10, Gal.5:22, Phil.4:4, 1 Peter 1:8, John 15:11, 1 John 1:4 - God is always there: Psalm 139, Is.43:2 - the joy of a good wife: Prov.18:22, Ec.9:9 - children a gift from God and a blessing: Psalm 127 - God's presence guaranteed and sufficient: Matt.28:18-20, Heb.4:12-16, 13:5-6

The beginning of wisdom

Only by putting God in His proper place in the whole scheme of things can the foundation be laid for properly understanding everything else. That's why the psalmist and the writer of Proverbs keep saying, "The fear of the Lord is the beginning of wisdom." If we try, as so many have, to understand our world and how it works without understanding how God fits into the picture, we wind up with confusion, not to mention a lack of meaning, with its accompanying despair. Without God, nothing makes sense, because He is the source of life and thus the source of sense about it.

With God in His proper place, which He has revealed to us abundantly through the Bible and through all of creation, everything else also fits and can be understood, at least as far as is humanly possible. With God in His proper place in the equation, things make sense, have meaning and purpose, with the accompanying sense of peace or satisfaction for the human mind and heart. It's only when we try to push Him aside, or leave Him out of the equation, that we experience bewilderment, feel lost and are continually searching for understanding and meaning. With that established, we can begin to understand.

The purpose of life

Down through the millenniums people have pondered the meaning or purpose of life, often at low points in their own lives. They have sought to justify their existence in many and varied ways. Though I have pondered it on and off for years, this question came to the fore with increased significance during the low point in my life – my midlife crisis.

Searching the Scriptures, I found no place where it said "the meaning or purpose of life is…" My normal course of action in such a situation is to leave the question in God's hands, knowing that He knows that I'm looking for an answer. My experience has been that this allows Him, as I do my ordinary Bible reading and meditation, to bring thoughts to my mind that will contribute to answering my question. The results of this process are outlined below.

God put all of His wisdom and ingenuity into creating life with all of its potential, to be realized as we share it with Him. He pronounced the result of this creativity to be good. In other words, the wisest and most loving Person in the universe thought it was a good idea. That thought kept me going through the darkest days of my midlife crisis. If that's not enough reason for living, consider this.

Things got challenging when our wrong choices dislocated everything and formed the root of most of the difficulties and heartaches that have become a standard part of our everyday lives. However, built into God's plan and brought to fruition in Jesus was a means of redemption, paid for by His suffering and death. In other words, the wisest and most loving Person in the universe still thinks it's a good idea, even with all the accompanying difficulties. If that is not a powerful enough declaration that life is worth having and living, consider this.

Jesus tells us that He will walk each step with us, if we'd like. He says we can share life with Him and participate in His wonderful, eternal plan. In other words, the wisest and most loving Person in the universe wants to share life with you and wants you to share His life. If that doesn't provide purpose and motivation for living, consider this.

Wanting to leave God out of the picture, people have tried all kinds of ways to find meaning or purpose without Him. They have tried everything – drugs, sex, and excitement, life-risking thrills, even trying to be good and serving others. The unanimous conclusion is that the best attempts fall far short without God. In other words, there is no other way, and they have all been tried.

So it all boils down to this: The purpose of life is to know God, to be an active participant in His eternal plan and to enjoy Him forever. I don't know how you could ever find a more awesome, vibrant and rewarding purpose than that. Go with it into each new day!

...and live happily ever after

When God brought His people out of bondage in Egypt and led them into the Promised Land (a picture of what He wants to do for each of us), He made them an extraordinary offer. He said that if they would follow Him, listening to His direction, He would give them all they needed to have a good life – good health, good crops, good weather, good homes, peace and security, good families, etc., etc. – in other words, they would live happily ever after. Then He demonstrated the validity of His offer by doing miraculous things for them which showed them He could keep His side of the deal.

But, incredibly, they turned down His offer. After He had brought them into the Promised Land, they decided they no longer wanted the deal, didn't want to live happily ever after. They wanted, instead, to do their own thing, go their own way, and follow gods of their own design, even though God had told them explicitly that He was judging the people of the land for that very reason. Think about it! Living happily ever after was not enough. Contentment, security and prosperity were not enough. So they traded them in for excitement, uncertainty, sin and death.

The offer still stands. Although the physical prosperity part does not apply in the same way in the Church Age, Jesus lived among us, died and rose again to offer us the opportunity to live happily ever after, to have "love, joy, peace, etc..." Incredibly, despite what we see in the history of the children of Israel, we still turn down His offer, for the most part. We, too, want to do our own thing, go our own way, and follow gods of our own design. We are willing to trade contentment for control, even though we know from experience that our choices don't often achieve what we want.

This conundrum throws the question of the purpose of life completely out of whack. We ask, "What is the point?" when what we really mean is "Why isn't this working out the way I want it to?" All the while we still try to do things our own way, rather than trying to find God's way. One definition of insanity is to do the same thing over and over, expecting a different result. To borrow a phrase from a song of my youth, "When will we ever learn? When will we ever learn?"

To find the purpose of life, we must truly look for it; not just keep up with trial and error and wonder why it's not working. In my experience, it's not that the purpose of life is some great mystery, because the Creator of life has explained it fairly simply, so that we can enjoy it. It's just that we don't want that explanation. We want to make up our own and then act baffled when it doesn't work, never fits with reality.

Again, the purpose of life is to know God, to be an active participant in His eternal plan and to enjoy Him forever. If you don't want that, you'll never understand the purpose of life, and nothing will ever work right. If you are willing to be content with that incredible offer, the purpose of life will be obvious, and you will live happily ever after.

Why is the world a mess?

Down through time this has been a perpetual question. If God is all-powerful, wise and loving, why is there so much evil in the world? On a more personal level, the question always seems to deteriorate into "Why do bad things happen to me?" When God should be getting the thanks for all the wonderful things He has created and is presently doing for each of us so graciously, instead He is getting blamed for all the bad things that happen to us, even the ones that are clearly our fault. As this is still a pressing and greatly misunderstood question for so many, let's consider an answer that God obviously understands and wants us to know in order to ease our troubled minds.

Our first glimpse of creation is an awesome one. A perfect world. A perfect atmosphere in a perfect setting. A perfect life lay out before them, stretching out into eternity. Looking at it from His perspective, God said it was "very good". So it's obvious that something must have changed. Something must have gone wrong for that perfect world to have degenerated into the troubled world we have known down through history. This change is the key to coming to grips with the mess in which we find ourselves, a mess that often results in confusion, as well as heartache.

So what happened? What changed? Part of God's creation of man in His image was the gift of the capacity for making decisions. Think of what a risk that was, the potential for the ruination of the perfect world He designed with us in mind! And yet, in order for us to be able to freely know and love Him in His fullness, He generously gave us that gift, with all of its ramifications.

He told Adam and Eve that they were to enjoy and care for His beautiful world, with only one condition, "Do not eat of the tree in the center of the garden". We all know the story, and we all would probably have done the same thing, since we all have at one time or another. At some point (the Bible does not tell us how long they enjoyed perfection); Adam and Eve decided that they wanted more. What God had given them was not enough or good enough. With only a slight nudge from an attractive snake, they decided to disobey God and eat of that tree.

Adam and Eve physically, emotionally and spiritually felt the resulting change in their world. Suddenly, they knew they were naked, and that now felt wrong. They became afraid of the most wonderful Person in the world and hid when He showed up for His usual evening visit. They knew that something was different in their relationship with God and, in their shame and confusion, began to make excuses when faced with His questions. They were overwhelmed by the change that had taken place, the change that opened the door to the mess with which we have had to deal ever since.

The results of that change are at least twofold. Besides losing out on a perfect world, wrong choices now became a way of life. Beginning rather dramatically with Cain's murder of Abel, the world saw about 1500 years of wickedness that led to the flood which destroyed all but one family.

Thoughts for Jesse

The second result was difficulty in decision making within the human heart that caused the prophet Jeremiah to declare, "The heart is deceitful above all things and desperately wicked: who can know it?" (so much for the wisdom of "following your heart".) Paul summed up this concept in the seventh chapter of Romans by saying, basically, "I don't do what I know is right, and I do what I know is wrong, and Jesus is the only one who can help me."

The outcome of the sum total of wrong choices by people down through time is the mess we find in the world today. People have persisted in making poor choices, in spite of God's clear presentation of the consequences and His constant admonition to choose wisely. The Bible is full of poor choices by the children of Israel, God's chosen, protected and personally guided people. And they were merely a publicly recorded example of the way we all are, which would leave us in a bind, if not for God's gracious plan of redemption.

But God did make provision for the mess to be dealt with, taking upon Himself the solution to the problem which we created. Redemption was paid for by Jesus' death and resurrection. It is offered to each of us personally by the Holy Spirit. And, for all those who receive it, that redemption is completed in the new heaven and new earth, where the perfection of the original creation will be restored.

However, until then, we are still in the midst of the mess, with all its heartache. Wickedness still seems prominent throughout the world, touching each of us in its way. My son, Jesse, was killed because people are

10

1 | The Purpose of Life

still making poor choices. In the midst of the mess, though, we can make a difference for the better by making wise choices with God's help and guidance, which He offers freely to all.

The hard part is that, in a way, the best we can expect is an approximation of life as God originally intended it to be. In other words, even on our best days we can expect bumps in the road, until that day when the rough will be made smooth, the effects of sin removed forever. This is not cause for discouragement, however, as God's grace is always sufficient for our present distresses, and His joy can be our constant portion, no matter how bumpy the road.

For example, consider what we are going through with the loss of Jesse. People keep talking about us getting back to "normal", whatever that is for anybody. But we will never get back to the old normal again. Our world is forever changed, by God's grace, for the better. As we walk with and trust Him, our new "normal" is deeper, fuller, a new level of existence. That's an incredible thought and even more incredible to experience in our darkest hour. Because of it, we can go on, in spite of the mess the world is in, find joy and life, and make a difference for the better. Awesome!

References: - creation perfect: Genesis 1-3, Romans 5:12, 17-21   - results of the fall: Genesis 6:5-13, Romans 7:15-25   - choices: Galatians 5:19-23   - God's admonitions: Joshua 24:14-28, Ezekiel 18:20-32   - Israel's pattern: Nehemiah 9:6-35   - redemption paid for: Romans 5:6-8,15-21   - redemption offered: John 10:10,

Romans 6:23, 2 Corinthians 5:17-19, 1 Timothy 2:3-6 -
redemption completed: Revelation 21-22 - your daily
choice: Galatians 5:16-25

Sharing the consequences

Sometimes we forget that we all must share the consequences of sin. We mistakenly think that, since Adam
and Eve were the actual ones who sinned, and thus
were responsible for the fall of man, that Adam and
Eve were the ones who had to bear the consequences of
that sin, that they, in fact, were the ones who deserved
it. We wonder why life is hard for us when they were the
ones who sinned, and we stagger on under the illusion
that we don't deserve the poor treatment life brings
our way.

Over the years I have come to the conclusion that
we all must share the consequences of sin, because, as
the Bible says, we all have sinned. As we each partake in
wrong choices, living in ways that we know are wrong,
if we would be honest with ourselves, we must not be
surprised when we have to bare the normal outcome of
those wrong choices. Even when we are doing our best,
we all must share the consequences of accumulated
human error, acknowledging that we have contributed
our share.

We are so subconsciously accustomed to this concept that we even have a common term for it. When

we've done our best, and things don't work out the way we hoped they would we say simply, "That's the way it goes." And we will continue to share the consequences of sin until redemption is complete, and sin is no more.

Life is too short...

A popular saying says "Life is too short to be unhappy." The Bible has a little different perspective on that thought: "So teach us to number our days, that we may apply our hearts unto wisdom" (Psalm 90:12). In other words, "Life is too short to be stupid."

Life is not fair...for whom?

We seem to have an ongoing fuss about how life is not fair and how terrible that is, especially when life is not fair to us personally. However, the reason for this is a little hard to face, because that is also very personal. We have a hard time with the reality that it might be our fault.

You see, life is unfair because we are unfair. In fact we want life to be unfair – in favor of us! We want bad things to only happen to other people, which is not fair. And if we were to play the lottery, where the chances of winning are millions to one, we think we should win, which is not fair to the other millions.

This outlook is not unusual. It's human nature. We want life to be weighted in our favor, and we are even willing to do shifty things to make it be that way, everything from telling little white lies to cheating on our taxes, both of which are not fair. But if it's not fair in our favor, we easily justify ourselves and even seek to perfect our sneaky methods to "get ahead".

This tendency, multiplied by ten billion, or however many people have ever lived, adds up to why life is unfair. And, as long as it's unfair in our favor, we heartily approve. It's only when we somehow get the short end of the stick (fair for somebody else), that we grumble and complain about how unfair life is.

We also tend to blame God, of all people, when our cumulated unfairness hits home. This seems patently unfair. Let's consider this concept in this way.

If you had a friend who was in difficulty of his own making, and you did everything you could to help, and he then blamed you for all his troubles, you would feel that that was terribly, unbelievably unfair. You would also wonder why you had even tried to help him. This, in a nutshell, is the position in which we have put God.

As we have already seen, most of our difficulties are directly or indirectly of our own making. God, out of His gracious concern, has gone to great lengths to help us, even to the extent of giving His own Son to die in our place to provide the way home. And what has been our response? Gratitude? Willingness to listen? Instead, we continue on our way with great grumbling and blame Him for our problems at every turn, the epitome of unfairness...for God.

The puzzle of life

When, in the Garden of Eden and ever since, we told God we'd rather do our own thing our own way, we lost the connection with God that He intended for us to have throughout our lives and on into eternity. One of the consequences of this poor choice was that we lost touch with who we are and with what we are here for. Life became a puzzle, rather than the walk in the light that God intended it to be.

So, during our lifetime, each of us must put together the puzzle that is our own life, and no one can do it for us. This used to be termed "finding your way", though the modern terminology is "finding yourself". Obviously, the best way to achieve that end is to begin by re-establishing that connection with God, so that He can help us, as per the original plan, but we each still have to put our own puzzle together.

This task is made more difficult by the obstacles that are both self-imposed and pressed upon us by the surrounding world. We begin with the hurdles of our own bad habits and dysfunctions, built in through our early life experiences. But then, as though these were not enough, the world around us seeks to move us in wrong directions. Peer pressure often urges wrong choices, even when we're trying to do right. The world pushes and pulls, offering temptations, thrills and excitement that we are told we would be foolish to pass up. These constantly challenge our sense of right and wrong and our resolve to do and be right.

In other words, that which is already difficult is made harder by the basic obstacle course of life itself. It's as though we are putting together a puzzle of paper pieces in a hurricane. It seems like everyone and everything is working against us, and few are helping. It becomes obvious that we need help from somewhere else, as the apostle Paul pointed out so poignantly in Romans, chapter seven, the description of his personal struggles. His conclusion? Only Jesus can give us victory.

God has made available all the resources we need for the task. He gives us His Word for knowledge, His Spirit for help, comfort and guidance, others for support and encouragement, and He gives us Himself daily. As a result, though the task seems daunting at times, it is also a fulfilling challenge as we work through it with Him.

References: - connection lost: Gen.3:22-24, Is.53:6, Rom.3:23, Rom.5:12 - connection restorable: Rom.5:8-11, 2 Cor.5:17-21, Eph.2:11-21 - resources available: the Word: Ps.19:7-11, 119:9, 11, 33-40, 105, John 17:17, 1 John 2:3-5   His Spirit: John 14:16-17, 26, 16:7-15, Gal.5:16-25, 6:7-8   others: Gal.6:1-2, Eph.4:11-16, Col.3:15-16, 1 John 1:3   Himself: Ps.18:30-32, John 14:21-23, Gal.2:20

The mystery of life

In addition to the puzzle of life, we also have to deal with the mystery of life. The puzzle of life refers to the problems we face in trying to decipher the path and purpose of our own individual lives. The mystery of life refers to the bigger picture, the comprehensive plan and purpose of God for life. A lack of some understanding of this latter concept is the cause of much confusion, disappointment and even despair. Conversely, coming to terms with it can bring peace of mind.

We must understand, to begin with, that this whole thing was God's idea, born out of a mind that is infinite in scope and possibility. The same Person Who thought all this up is the One Who said, "My ways and My thoughts are higher than your ways and your thoughts", intimating that we cannot hope to even come close to truly understanding what's involved in the creation and God's plan for it. He simply explained to us the things we need to know to be able to understand our part in the larger scheme of things. He expects us to leave the rest to His capable planning and care. As an unnecessary bonus, He allows us to get to know Him well enough to know that He is competent and trustworthy. We can approach each new day with the assurance that He not only knows what is going on but is able to handle any eventuality. His design in this is to enable us to live in peace, leaving the worrying to Him.

Consider the plan of redemption, which God has been working on and man has been worrying about for thousands of years. The evening after the fall disrupted God's beautiful creation, He promised redemption. People, in their short-range mindset, thought that would probably happen sometime in the next few days or weeks at the most. They were disturbed and impatient when God didn't even give them a time frame until Daniel's day, when He said the Messiah would show up in 500 years or so. 500 years!? Who can or even wants to operate in that kind of time frame?

And that's where some of the concept of impatience originates. By the time 500 years had passed, although they knew the birthplace, few people seemed to care that the Messiah had finally arrived. When Jesus began His public ministry, not fitting the proper, hoped-for pattern, people seemed to spend more time proving why He couldn't be the Messiah than embracing the redemption He brought.

This example epitomizes the mystery of life. With God's plans and purposes so far beyond our comprehension, we still think we should be able to understand them and make them fit into our very limited framework or else we'll complain, often bitterly, that it's just not fair and that we are being poorly treated somehow, even though we don't understand what's really happening or should be happening anyway. We wind up like little children whining about the unfairness of not being able to play in traffic, without even a thought that our parents might have a reasonable explanation that presently eludes our understanding. Like our parents in that situation, God is not particularly irritated with our childish complaining and does not feel compelled to explain everything. He simply continues to faithfully care for us until the day when we'll understand more fully.

So, for now, we need to just trust Him with the things we don't understand. We can take it for granted that there will be some of those and just leave them with Him; the One Who is so trustworthy and loving. Leaving them with Him allows Him to give us His peace as He continues to work all things out for our good within His perfect plan. What more could you ask for than God's best? Awesome!

Dad's philosophy of life (verbalized after 50 years of life, 33 years of knowing the Lord, 25 years of marriage, 23 years of parenting, 3 years of midlife crisis and 20 years of pastoring)

The apostle Paul often refers to life within a sports framework – running a race, striving to finish well, etc. After years of playing and coaching sports, it has helped my understanding to view life as a game. A game with serious aspects and consequences, but a game, nonetheless, to strive at and to enjoy and to finish well. A game of independent action and results. A game of teamwork with others. A game of dependent working with God, the Coach and Source of all resources needed to play well.

With all this in mind, and with years of choosing teams at recess behind me, my philosophy of life boils down to this response to God: "Thanks for letting me play. Help me to play and finish well, for You and for those around me."

The overview of history (see also free will)

Make no mistake. God Almighty, the Creator and Ruler of the universe has complete and absolute control of the course of history. He knows the end from the beginning, and His plan shall not fail. It most assuredly will be accomplished. Redemption was prophesied and fulfilled. Christ's kingdom is prophesied and will be brought to pass. Judgment and the ultimate victory of righteousness are prophesied, and we will each personally see its implementation.

With that foundation for history, we look at man's part. Down through the years, different cultures and people are given the opportunity to take the lead on the world stage to complement Israel. The millenniums have seen Egypt, Assyria, and Babylon... Persia, Darius, Cyrus...Alexander, Rome...China, Mongols, Ottomans...Britain, Hitler, and Communism all come and go. The United States currently has the lead. God allows these to move history and people and to accomplish things while they are concurrently accomplishing His purposes, such as bringing judgment or setting the stage for other people or events.

All of these have to meet God's conditions for leadership and face judgment for failure. (1 Kings 14:7-16) Thus, some have lasted longer than others. For all of them, though, their accomplishments mainly wind up as museum pieces or piles of rocks around the world. When people have had their turn, then God will have His, and many powerful empires are now simply brief notes in history books.

Throughout history, Israel has been the public example of how God deals with people, in all of their positive and negative aspects. Occasionally, God sent someone along, like Josiah, to show how it could work, so there was never any excuse for failure. Because of His covenant with His friend Abraham, God never destroyed the nation of Israel, although they certainly deserved it at times and were severely chastened. The ultimate fulfillment of that covenant is still to come and will surely be accomplished by God's power and in His time.

The Garden of Eden revisited

In a not so different way, the sixties in the United States was the Garden of Eden revisited. People living in a postwar paradise decided that what they had was not good enough. As though tempted by the old serpent himself, they decided, contrary to revealed truth and fundamental logic, to do their own thing, regardless of the consequences. They began to eat of every forbidden fruit they could find, and when those weren't exciting enough, they made up some new ones.

The results of such self-gratification were similar to those in the Garden -- all downhill, for themselves, their families, their communities and their country. Through a lifestyle of which they were defiantly proud, they ushered in an era similar to that after the fall, an era of violence, sexual perversity, anarchy and fragmentation of society. We have yet to see the long range effects, although, if the original Garden of Eden scenario is any indication, we have a hard road ahead.

A matter of focus

In the beginning... in the beauty and wonder of the Garden of Eden, the focus was on knowing God and on eternity, very farsighted. Adam and Eve had just been given life that was intended to last forever. They could eat from the tree of life whenever they wanted to, so they understood that there was no end in sight. God came to them in the cool of the evening to visit, to share their life and to share His life with them. Things could not have been better. The outlook could not have been better, stretching off into the distance as far as they could imagine. Then the focus changed.

The most nearsighted person in history convinced them to be nearsighted, too. Taking their eyes off God and eternity, they focused on their immediate surrounding, the tree of the knowledge of good and evil, a false promise of better things than God could provide. In so doing, they lost sight of eternity, and, since then, we have been focused on the immediate pleasure and pain, life and death, with no regard for eternal consequences, either positive or negative.

We focus on the pursuit of pleasure with no thought for the results. We focus on problems and pain with no thought about how they fit into God's eternal plan and purpose. In becoming so shortsighted, we lose touch with significance, even though God has continually sought to call us out of the temporal and into the eternal.

When Jesus came to reconcile us to God, He called us back into contact with eternity. He said, "Seek ye first the kingdom of God and His righteousness, and all these things (the temporal things we tend to focus on) shall be added unto you." In other words, get back in touch with eternity, and the immediate will fall into place as a natural result. He goes on to say elsewhere, "This is life eternal, that they may know You, the only true God, and Jesus Christ, whom You have sent." Reconnecting with the eternal God puts everything else into its proper perspective.

Paul, a man who suffered as much as any man, reminds us of this principle when we are dealing with tribulation, telling us to put tough times into an eternal perspective. In that light, they are but a short-term problem with an eternal benefit. Then he admonishes us to look at things that are not seen, because they are eternal, rather than at things that are seen, because they are only temporal.

From this perspective temporal pleasures have less significance. Problems and pain acquire purpose in God's plan. It's all a matter of the proper focus.

Chapter two

Marriage

MARRIAGE WAS DESIGNED BY GOD to bless the earth and its people. Done properly, marriage is a taste of heaven. We lose sight of its value when we focus solely on its physical or procreative side. Marriage is the building block of society, a safe place to be and to grow as we face the rest of life.

We say, "Behind every successful man is a good woman", but it works both ways. God gave us marriage as an encouragement and support system to help each of us to be all that we were meant to be. And it's first about taking us outside of ourselves to focus on the needs of another, to learn to be unselfish, giving and loving on a daily basis, lessons we need for all of life.

Marriage is about enjoying each other, not about fixing each other. In a culture filled with self-help books, seminars, and DVDs, we presume it is our job to fix each other, and when we live with someone we assume the role of personal trainer, therapist and counselor, to the annoyance of our spouse. However, each of us already wants to be a better person, especially for someone we love; so if we would simply enjoy each other, encourage each other and support each other we would have much more fun, and the results would be growth together. We grow more easily in order to please the other, rather than to obey them.

Some basic concepts for marriage

The only good foundation for marriage is commitment. Physical attraction changes. "Love" waxes and wanes. Compatibility changes as people change. Everything the world tries to base a marriage upon is changeable and probably will; which is why couples often say, "We have grown apart." Commitment to each other is the only thing which will keep you growing together, doing whatever it takes to strengthen your marriage. This is why the marriage ceremony includes the words, "Will you…?" It's a choice, a commitment. You may fall in love; but marriage is a commitment to stay there.

This concept is so unique and so strong that I am of the opinion that any man can have a good marriage with any woman, if they are both willing to love, to make it work. In fact, the Bible never says to marry the one you love. It spends all its time on teaching us to love the one we marry.

This is also why I counsel young people to marry a nice person. An attractive person who is not nice will gradually become more and more unattractive. A nice person will grow more and more attractive as you share a commitment to learn to love each other.

The inner beauty will rise to the surface within the context of commitment.

Ephesians 5:21-33 is a beautiful picture of God's idea of marriage. Although too often it is misused to make the husband the boss, the passage actually begins with the concept of submitting to each other. Different responsibilities are given to each – the husband is to love, and the wife is to respect – but the main idea is that you are supposed to live for each other. And it's easy to live for someone who is living for you. In fact, properly applied, this passage makes marriage the closest thing to heaven we have on this earth.

The number one priority in a marriage is maintenance. This sounds a little funny at first, but think about it. Nothing in this life survives without maintenance. Why should we think that marriage would? When a red light comes on on the dash of our car, we attend to the problem before something blows. When we come into a room and notice our spouse has a red light on (if you've been together long, you know what I'm talking about), attend to the problem right away, or something is going to blow. If you do that along with your regular maintenance schedule, your car and your marriage will run smoothly for a long time.

Love redefined

In the beginning love had a simple definition. Love was intimate fellowship with God in all the joy and beauty of a flawless creation. His incredible care was evident everywhere they looked, filling their experience. His love was so much a part of their everyday existence that they just enjoyed it, took it for granted, didn't need to examine or question or define it.

Then sin, sorrow and death came into the world as a result of their own choices. Fellowship with God was seriously disrupted, and now love was redefined, bearing few of the former characteristics. Without God's love to define and exemplify what it should be, love was redefined in terms of lust, physical attraction, and warm fuzzy feelings, with the attending confusions about what it really is or if we really love someone. So many times, a couple comes for counseling, says they don't love each other any more, and yet can't give a good definition of love when asked. So how do they know they don't love each other any more, I wonder?

One of the questions on my pre-marriage homework is "What is love?", and through the years this has consistently been the one couples have had the most problems with, simply coming up with a practical working definition. One girl asked her colleagues at work, and they didn't know either. So I get definitions out of popular songs or movies, ideas about warm fuzzy feelings or birds singing on a summer day whenever they are close to each other.

With such an ethereal concept, is it any wonder that it doesn't last? That there aren't always birds singing when things get tough? That it's not warm when you're tired or cranky? To truly experience love, we need to redefine it properly.

The Bible speaks extensively about what love does, summed up nicely in the love chapter, 1 Corinthians 13. However, I have only found one place, 2 John 6, which gives what may be considered a definition of love. It says loves is obedience to the Word in relation to another person. In other words, love is truth-based caring, always doing what is right for the other person. Ordinarily, feelings will follow along with the actions, since this is God's idea of love.

This also says that love is a choice, which is a good thing. This means that you can love your spouse even when you don't feel like it. And 1 John 2:5 says that feelings will come into line when you do the right things, when you do what love does.

All this to say that when we bring God back into the definition, love comes out right again. When His kind of love guides us, we learn how to love each other. With His involvement in our lives and love, His truth naturally guides us into His kind of love, which is always stronger and purer than anything we can manufacture ourselves. This is the kind of love we long for, a love which will endure and will sustain our joy in our relationship.

Love fulfills life, marriage and the law

Creation began in the Spirit, filled with love and fueled by love. Then Adam and Eve chose an alternate route, chose to do their own thing in their own wisdom and strength. The resulting fall also resulted in man losing the power and grace of love and the Spirit. The outcome – the rule of the flesh – quickly degenerated into chaos and wickedness that led to the judgment of God in the flood.

To help bring order and discipline to the flesh and the world, God gave us the law, which also demonstrated our need for redemption, pointing the way to Christ, the Saviour. When He came, he opened the way, through His death and resurrection, to the opportunity for a return to the realm of the Spirit, filled and fueled by love. People had a tendency to begin along that road, then get uncomfortable with it, being used to walking in the flesh, and return to the old way, depending on their own wisdom and strength, looking to the law and legalism to bring security and a comfortable place to be.

In Galatians, God calls us away from that path and back to the way of love and the Spirit. In Romans 13:10 the Bible tells us that love – always doing what's right for another – is the fulfillment of the law. Galatians 5 tells us that the way of the Spirit is the way of love and thus is the fulfillment of the law. So you can try to do what's right by following the law, which is weak in that we are weak. Or you can follow the Spirit Who leads us into love, which naturally results in doing what's right for others.

Galatians also tells us that this is the path of liberty, unbound by the law, free to follow the Spirit Who leads us into love which fulfills the law. The freedom in the Spirit also includes joy, peace, longsuffering, kindness, goodness, etc., which are hard to achieve through legalism. Thus, Spirit-empowered love is the way to go for fulfillment of the law, fulfillment in life, and fulfillment in marriage. And it's a lot funner.

A few collected words of wisdom for marriage

- Remember to enjoy each other.

- Focus on what you like about each other, rather than on the negatives.

- Rediscover each other once in a while.

- Time and energy spent on your marriage is an investment that will bring dividends and are never wasted.

- Always assume the best while figuring out the rest.

- Getting closer to God together will bring you closer to each other.

- Establish healthy habits together early, but it's never too late to start.

- Remember you are a team, not opponents.

- You can't hurt the other without hurting yourself. You can't help the other without helping yourself.

- Practice kindly honesty.

- Do not both be mad at the same time. And never go to bed angry.

- Whether you think you can make this marriage work or whether you think you can't, you're right.

- Always remember simple courtesies.

- When asked on his fiftieth anniversary, one older gentleman said the secret of long marriage was a bad memory, a unique way of reminding us not to hold grudges or to continually bring up past mistakes or problems.

- Bring flowers or other special treats on days that you're not expected to.

- Don't let problems linger. Work things through before they become overwhelming, and move on with resolution as a building block for future growth and problem solving together.

- It is your seemingly opposite qualities which make you a more complete, whole and efficient couple. Ruth Graham said, "If you agree on everything, one of you is unnecessary." So enjoy each others' differences, as well.

They are probably what attracted you to each other to begin with.

Love and the gifts of the Spirit

1 Corinthians 13 being in the middle of the chapters on the gifts of the Spirit tells us the relationship between love and the gifts. The gifts are designed as tools to help us with love, which is the most important thing. The gifts will pass away, but love is eternal. If we are not using the gifts to grow in love, we are misusing them.

Chapter three

Divorce and Remarriage

GOD HATES DIVORCE! ANY DISCUSSION of divorce and remarriage must begin with that foundational thought. ***God hates divorce!*** It messes up His plan for joy and blessing and ushers in so much pain and problems. It breaks up homes and families, communities and countries and wreaks havoc in people's lives, especially children, who are precious in His sight. So we must begin there if we are to understand concepts, concerns and the practical considerations of divorce and remarriage. By the way, if you are divorced, you have experienced the pain and should even now be nodding in agreement and reading on to see God's provision for your situation.

There are reasons for divorce, of which infidelity is not one, although it's the most popular "biblical" reason given. The Bible passage most often quoted to support this justification of divorce actually addresses the situation in which someone is unfaithful before marriage (fornication). In fact, as the story of Joseph and Mary illustrates, the unfaithful one *must* be put away to preserve the integrity of Jewish society. But there is no other place or setting in the Bible where this situation is given as grounds for divorce, though we often use it as a basis for not dealing with a difficult situation.

Infidelity indicates serious underlying problems, and the Bible calls us to address those problems and rebuild the marriage, not discard it. Actually, there is no marriage problem which cannot be solved if both parties are willing. If couples would spend as much time and effort on resolving their problems as they do on divorce, they would find their love rekindled and their marriage rebuilt stronger then ever.

In my experience, divorce is ordinarily not because of an insurmountable problem, but simply because one or both don't want to be married any longer. Perhaps they have found someone else or it's simply too hard to work things out. Divorce is an easy way out. Jesus says this is just legalized adultery, to divorce one to marry another, and He disapproved strongly.

Jesus also mentioned that God told Moses to legalize divorce, but only because of the hardness of their hearts. Before that, men were simply discarding women to marry others, which left the discarded women at a great disadvantage. A bill of divorcement at least gave them legal standing to be remarried and provided for. However, this would not even be necessary except for the hardness of heart which caused them to make wrong choices to begin with and to have no consideration for the needs of the discarded woman.

In looking out for women, God said the men **had** to give them a bill of divorcement, so they were not left stranded financially, physically and emotionally in a society that had no means of provision for a woman without any legal status. God's plan gave discarded women legal status and the right to remarry, so they could be provided for within a legal framework in that society. It was not designed as a basis for legalizing adultery, as Jesus pointed out (to the dismay of His male listeners).

So we see the biblical concept of God's concern for and provision for the "innocent" party, a well-known characteristic of our heavenly Father. The Bible goes on to say that a believer is not under bondage if an unbeliever wants a divorce, although the believer should seek to work things out before marrying another, as the unbeliever's salvation may be at stake. The believer should be cautious, as well, about using this biblical provision as a means of legalized adultery. Unbelievers are not the only ones who abuse the law and use it for selfish purposes.

Another reason for divorce is physical abuse. However, there are many things a wife can do to protect herself and her children that would have a positive effect on the marriage, and she should first seek help along those lines. Divorce should not be the first option. As with any tough situation in marriage, the initial effort should be to address the problems and work things out, although, as I have already stated, I realize that is not always possible. The woman should seek safety first, then find help to resolve the underlying problems in the marriage, before she even considers divorce.

Thus we see that there are very few biblical grounds for divorce and very many biblical instructions for working on marriage. And God provides all the resources needed to do that, if people are willing. God also knows that there are times when people simply are not willing to work on their marriage, and He has made provision for the innocent party, as they honestly look to Him for help, wisdom and guidance.

With all these foundational principles in mind, and they are each important as a basis for decision making, the "innocent" party is free to remarry. No one is ever completely innocent, but if one has done their best, God's forgiveness is available. The marriage vow has been broken by the other, and the innocent party is no longer under obligation to that.

Being free to remarry is not the same thing as being easy to marry however. There will always be baggage and scars, although the Lord's healing grace is compassionate and kind. Hopefully, the wounded party will be able to go cautiously and wisely into a new marriage, armed with the painful lessons learned, and experience God's grace in that relationship.

References: - God hates divorce: Mat.5:31-32, 19:4-6 - divorce for fornication: Deut.22:13-21 - address marriage problems: 1 Cor.7:10-11 - Jesus' feelings about legalized adultery: Matt.5:31-32 - hardness of heart: Matt.19:8- bill of divorce required: Deut.24:1-2 - male dismay: Matt.19:10 - believer's responsibility: 1 Cor.7:10-16, 1 Peter 3:1-4 - working on marriage: 1 Cor.7:10-16, Eph.5:21-33, Col.3:18-19, 1 Peter 3:1-9 - no more obligation: 1Cor.7:15

Chapter four

The Purpose of the Church

THERE IS A MISUNDERSTANDING ABOUT the relationship of the church and Israel, based on the idea that when Israel was set aside, the church took her place and inherited all the promises. This is wishful thinking with no basis in Scripture. God's covenant with Israel still stands, and He will fulfill all His promises to her. The church is not simply a replacement Israel.

This is why you always find Israel in the middle of any end times teaching in the Bible. In the last days, God, by His power and mercy, gathers Israel from the ends of the earth, gives them a new heart and mind to follow Him, establishes Jesus (in fulfillment of His promise to David) on the throne as king of Israel, and once again gives Israel a prominent place on earth, as His chosen people to bless all others. There are promises yet to come for Israel, and God will fulfill every one, because He is a promise keeping God.

Israel was set aside temporarily because of sin and persistent disobedience; so God needed someone to take her place in the work He had given her to do – to be His representative in the world. He established the church for this purpose, with its own set of promises, purposes and empowerments. He never promised the church, as He did Israel, that she would drive out her enemies, occupy their land, and become rich and fat. He promised the church tribulation, answered prayer, the fullness of the Spirit, and His constant presence as it shared the gospel to the ends of the earth.

The point was to prevent the church from getting settled into comfortable friendship with this world. We are to be in the world, but not of the world. We are to share the same response that Jesus got, hated by those who would have hated Him, listened to by those who would have listened to Him. Our citizenship is in heaven, and we need to represent Him well down here until He calls us home. We are not to be concerned with building a legacy here, but to be laying up treasure in heaven. We are to be seeking first the kingdom of God and His righteousness and allowing Him to look after all the rest. This understanding would prevent much of the confusion and misplaced expectations we see in the church today.

References - Israel gathered and given a new heart: Ezekiel 36:21-38 - David's descendant to be king: 2 Sam.7:13-16, Rev.20:4 - promises to the church: John16:33, John 17:7, Acts 1:8, Matt.28:18-20 - in, not of, the world: John 17:11,15 - received like Jesus: John 15:20 - heavenly citizenship: Eph.2:18-22, Heb.12:22-23 - laying up treasure in heaven: Matt.6:19-21 - our priority: Matt.6:33

Basis blueprint for the church

Imagine, for a moment, that Jesus came back for a visit. He gets all the church leaders in the world together and asks them, "What have you done with My church?" And they come forward one by one to tell Him the wonderful things they have done for Him with His church.

They would tell Him how they have organized things so the church can be more effective and efficient. They would explain their worship formats which have made the church more relevant to their culture and more accessible to all. They would explain how they got so big or why they stayed so small. They would tell Him all the things they have done for Him.

When each has had their turn, Jesus would say, "That's nice. It seems like you've done good things with My church…as long as you have followed the basic blueprint I gave you."

And they would say, "What blueprint?"

They would ask that question because, as far as they knew, Jesus never gave a blueprint for the church. And the reason they think that is because few have ever looked for His blueprint for the church. This is entirely understandable, since Jesus never talked much about the church. It was after His time, beginning on Pentecost with the coming of the Holy Spirit. Then you begin to hear about the church.

But the church is His body, and surely He knew it was coming and had planned for it. And if He had planned for it, surely He gave to His followers, who would be the church, a blueprint for it, something to guide them when He was gone. Operating under that assumption, I began to look for it, and I found it in the fifteenth chapter of John, right in the midst of His final instructions to His disciples before His death. It looks something like this...

It begins with an important foundational thought. Abide in Me. Abide in Me. Abide in Me. He says that over and over in several different ways. Abide in Me. In other words, we are supposed to be doing church *with* Him, not for Him. He even goes so far as to say that if we miss this principle, then we can do nothing, nothing of substance, nothing of lasting value, nothing of any worth to Him or to us.

I heard a preacher raise the question this way, "If Jesus did not come to our worship service, would we notice?" A penetrating question, but one that challenges everything we do with church or in church. He is the head of the church, the life of the church, the reason for the church. Let us make sure we are doing church with Him.

Let me summarize the rest of what I found in John 15 as the basic blueprint of the church – the church is friends of Jesus who gather to get to know Him better, to support one another, and to prepare to share His message with the world.

As Jesus lays the blueprint for the church, He changes the relationship between Himself and His disciples. He said He didn't call them servants anymore, but rather, He called them friends, friends He would give His life for, friends He would share everything with;

friends He would expect to share everything with Him. This is a pleasant and uplifting approach to church, one that constantly draws us to Him.

When we gather, our friendship with Him is the underlying motivation. We want to get to know Him through His Word. We want to lean on Him. We want to learn to love Him. We want to do what He teaches us so we can share His joy. We want our friendship to be clean and pure, faithful and strong.

He next reminds them that church is where we gather as friends of Jesus to support each other. He commands them to love each other, as He has loved them. As He speaks of the work He has given them to do, He reminds them that they are in it together, the support they need to do that work together.

Then He emphasizes their purpose, to share His message with the world. He has given them His Word and His love, His example and His Spirit and their support for one another to enable them to be His "branches", to speak for Him the message the world needs to hear. He has chosen them for that purpose. He taught and trained and empowered them for that job. They can access the Father's provision for that. As His motivation had been to "be about My Father's business", so He expected them (and us) to carry on with that work. We acquire much of what we need for that when we gather as the church.

That blueprint has served the church well for two thousand years through all cultures and locations. It has transcended time and place, because Jesus transcends time and place. We would do well to stick to that blueprint as we look to the day when the Head of the church returns to receive His own.

An additional thought from the end of Acts 2, in which we watch the birth of the church with over three thousand joining them that first day. We find that the church is to be the incubator where new believers can grow in warmth and safety to prepare to face the world on their own. It is a place where they can begin to grow, nurtured by the teaching of the Word and by fellowship with other believers and with Jesus, the Head of the church. They are to be welcomed into the church and into our homes to share the breaking of bread and a safe place to learn and grow in becoming friends with Jesus among other friends of Jesus. He must always be our focus if we are to nurture the young.

So let us do church with Jesus. Let us focus always on our friendship with Him. Let us nurture new believers and support each other in the things that come our way. And let us be diligent in doing the work He has given us to do – sharing the gospel with the world. Then we will be unashamed when the Head of the church comes for His own.

Game plan for the church

Ironically, the game plan for the church is summed up best in John 3:16, a verse usually used to say God loves me, and in Ephesians 4, a passage often used to outline the process for the perfection of self within the church. John 3:16 begins with the main viewpoint that God loved *the world*. Everything He does is with that thought in mind. This is the reason He sent His Son, not just because He loves *me*. Then He moves to how that gift can redeem the world – anyone, everyone, whosoever, receives that gift will be saved. God planned it. Jesus paid for it. The church has the responsibility to carry the plan to whosoever; so they can believe. That's the game plan.

Paul picks up on that game plan in Ephesians 4 when he explains how Jesus has gifted the church to carry out the ministry of redemption in the world. He addresses the different responsibilities we have and the attitude we should have to be able to do that properly. He talks about how our lives should be changed and changing for the church to be operating smoothly in carrying out the game plan. He continually focuses our attention on the priority of effective ministry of the church to be doing what Jesus gave us to do. So we need to continually lift our focus above self to serve others, as this is the purpose of the church.

Chapter five

The Secret of Prayer

DOWN THROUGH THE MILLENNIUMS, PEOPLE have cast a wistful eye on the numberless resources at God's disposal, "the cattle on a thousand hills". To many, that bounty appeared to be like a giant checking account just waiting to be accessed, if only one could figure out the secret, the secret of prayer. If only we could get on God's good side, learn what buttons to push, decipher the code or find someone who held the key that would open the door to such wealth and blessing.

American culture, the American dream of wealth and the good life, has caused the search to intensify. Significant and insignificant prayers in the Bible have been examined and re-examined ad nauseum. Jesus has been studied as the ultimate Insider in the realm of access to God through prayer. People have pored over Scriptures, prayed for insight, developed theories, written books and given seminars that made them some money and gained some followers, and yet...the secret has never been satisfactorily explained that will enable the ordinary citizen to share the bounty. So, what are we missing? What stone has been left unturned? Why has no one found a way to get what we want? To access the limitless storehouse of the riches of God?

The answer is so simple that it is exasperating. There is no secret! There is merely a monumental misunderstanding of what prayer is all about, which explains the confusion. When you go looking for an answer that isn't there, obviously you're never going to find it. Before some reader freaks out at this point, let me explain.

PRAYER IS NOT ABOUT GETTING THINGS! That was written in my best booming, Charlton Heston, voice of God intonation. And that wasn't loud enough. It wasn't powerful enough. That doesn't even begin to express years of pent up frustration over this matter. So, watch out!

Are we so incredibly selfish and self-centered as to think that the purpose of prayer is to get things?! Whether it's selfish things like health and wealth and happiness, or "unselfish things" like people being helped or saved, this mentality still boils down to getting things. It still boils down to "how do we access the power and riches of God for our benefit?" How egocentric! How shallow! How shortsighted! How idiotic! I'm running out of terms of incredulity here.

I repeat PRAYER IS NOT ABOUT GETTING THINGS! Prayer is simply the communication link in our relationship with God, part of the means of understanding His leading and then providing the resources to follow that leading. And there is no secret to that. Since this is so vital to our life and our eternity, God has made it open and plain to all. God wants everyone to know and have access to His plans and resources for life. Being totally unselfish, He offers this freely to all.

God shares His heart with us when He addresses the issue this way before He takes the children of Israel into the promised land, "Oh, that there were such a heart in them, that they would fear Me, and keep all My commandments always, that it might be well with them, and with their children forever!" Paul says it like this, "He that spared not His own Son, but delivered Him up for us all, how shall He not with Him also freely give us all things?" Jesus, the ultimate Insider, explains it this way, "Seek first the kingdom of God and His righteousness, and all these things shall be added unto you," and "If you abide in Me, and My words abide in you, you shall ask what you will, and it shall be done unto you." Prayer is part of a living relationship, not simply access to a cosmic vending machine.

As a rather ironic side note, we look briefly here at how to pray, ironic in that there is so little in the Bible by way of instruction in this seemingly most basic of points on prayer. You would think that God would have given Adam and Eve at least a short lesson on how to pray, what to say and how to say it when addressing Him, the Creator and Lord of the universe and of their lives. But, no. All we see is conversation in the cool of the evening, with no recorded instruction whatsoever, which leads us to one of two conclusions. Either the most important part of their relationship with God was supposed to be a mystery or all that was required was what came naturally. As you will see as we proceed, I'm highly inclined toward the latter.

In fact, until we get to the book of Psalms, there is nothing given that even resembles written instructions concerning what prayer might look like, and then only casually, almost accidentally, as we glimpse how the Psalmists approach God. This is such a problem that we see the disciples, some 4000 years into human history, finally faced with Jesus, God in the flesh, asking Him early on to teach them how to pray, as though that is not part of their primary lessons in elementary synagogue classes, as one might suppose it should be. In our own childhoods, we are taught, not how to pray, but rather just some simple prayers to say – "Now I lay me down..." and "God is great. God is good..." So we face life without basic instruction in what is perhaps the most vital resource for dealing with life and what it brings our way.

This brings us back to the two possible conclusions from the Garden of Eden: either the most important part of our relationship with God is supposed to be a mystery or all that is required is what comes naturally from our heart's response to our Creator. In other words, just as God didn't give them or us instructions on breathing because those instructions are so vital that they are instinctive, built in, so God doesn't need to give us instructions on prayer because those instructions are so vital that they are instinctive, built in. When even a professed atheist finds himself in deep trouble, the natural, instinctive cry of the heart is, "God, help me." It is inside us already to cry out to God when we need help, and that's fine with Him, because He put that instinct there. When we have a narrow escape, our instinctive response is, "Thank God!" When we have some uplifting experience it's natural to lift our heart in praise to God. It's not so much that we need instructions on prayer as that we can't keep from praying. It's not the form or the format that is important in prayer, but the condition of the heart in seeking to relate to the heart of God. Let's consider some examples.

We can basically choose any Bible person's life to illustrate how prayer is relational, in a way that's hopefully representative, but let's start the ball rolling with Enoch, obviously an intimate friend of God's. He should offer us significant insight into what it should be like to pray, what we should and shouldn't say, how to get what we want. And yet there is no record of any such prayers. Enoch's life is summed up by saying, "he walked with God" and "he pleased God". Since God took him home early, that was apparently what God was looking for, just that kind of relationship, which we also can offer Him.

Then there's Abraham, who, in periods of transition, danger and decisions, clearly needed to get answers to prayer, so his approach to God should be very instructive. We actually have records of some of his prayers, but his life is summed up by this sentence, "Abraham believed God, and it was imputed unto him for righteousness: and he was called the Friend of God." In other words, the basis for Abraham's prayer life was faith and an intimate relationship or friendship with God, rather than a desire to get things. As a result, Abraham's prayers were more of a give and take in his relationship with a Friend, rather than just requests for things he needed.

For example, in his prayer for Sodom, we see a conversation between Abraham and God that changes direction, developing as Abraham thinks through things while talking with God about them. He obviously feels free to think out loud in prayer, willing to face reality in his own mind and gradually realizing that God's intention is fully justified. However, God still takes Abraham's request under advisement and apparently would have done what Abraham asked, if Abraham's conditions were met by the Sodomites. This is a fairly common scenario in discussions between friends, a discussion, by the way, that was initiated by God Himself to allow Abraham the opportunity to be involved in the solution to Sodom's problem, since Abraham had family members who would be directly affected by the decisions made.

This example adds a new dimension to the idea of prayer, the concept that prayer can be a discussion with God, an examination of different sides of the issue at hand, rather than just the presentation of a request. If this is any indication of God's view of prayer, this is something which we should look into more fully, as this would completely alter our approach to prayer. If prayer is about examining a problem, an issue, a plan or an event with the intent of finding the best solution with God's input and assistance, this would require major adjustments in our attitude and methodology.

God-initiated prayer is not unusual. When He felt like destroying the children of Israel for their disobedience and foolishness at Mt. Sinai, God brought Moses into the discussion. He told Moses that He was thinking of starting over with just Moses' family, and Moses intuitively understood that he was being given the opportunity to share his thoughts on the matter. Feeling free to enter into the discussion, Moses spoke what was on his mind, an interesting version of prayer. As we look at the psalmist's account of the incident, it seems obvious that Moses' opinion was the deciding factor in God *not* destroying the rebellious children of Israel.

This is an interesting example, of which there are several others throughout the Scriptures, that, though not always the deciding factor, God is interested in our opinion. And we see, time and again, that God will even accommodate our ideas into His final actions without feeling that His sovereignty is threatened. He is even willing to change the course of history at our suggestion, as He is able to accomplish His will in any number of ways.

He was willing to spare Sodom and Gomorrah at Abraham's suggestion that there might be ten righteous people there; although it turned out He could only find 1½. He was willing to spare all of the children of Israel at Moses' request; although most of them later died in the wilderness when they refused to go into the promised land. As a loving father invites his children's input and makes adjustments accordingly, knowing that he can make everything come out right in the end; so our Heavenly Father does with us, to encourage us, to teach us, and to give us a chance to be involved in a real way.

In a way, when Jesus admonishes us to "ask...seek... and knock", He is initiating prayer and inviting us to participate in an exploration of God's will for a particular situation. Just as a child in a store asks Dad for something and through that means finds out the father's will, so God invites us to ask, as a means of finding out His will and as a means of learning about His will . When we see prayer as a discussion, rather than a request, it becomes part of the process in the growth of our relationship with God instead of being a means of blessing or disappointment, depending upon whether or not we get what we ask for. If we have the "not my will, but Yours be done" mindset of Jesus, finding and doing God's will is our chief concern, anyway, so this approach to prayer makes perfect sense.

Another example of this dimension of prayer is seen when Joshua, on the eve of a critical battle, encounters a warrior angel, sword in hand. When Joshua asks him whether he is on their side or on their enemies' side, the angel answers, "No, I come as the captain of the Lord's host." The angel was on God's side, there to accomplish God's plan in the battle. He was not open to manipulation from either side, though he was willing to answer Joshua's question. In other words, part of prayer is about being on God's side, rather than trying to get Him to be on your side.

Even Abraham Lincoln, though not known for his spirituality, understood that principle. When asked whether he thought God was on his side during the Civil War, he replied that the most important consideration was whether or not he was on God's side.

He evidently prayed often during the course of the war, but came to the conclusion that God would have His way in His time, and he should do his best to be a part of God's plan.

This concept gives direction to our praying, encouraging us to seek God's plan, rather than telling Him what to do. With Joshua (and Abraham Lincoln), we can be confident, knowing that God is in charge, competent to do the best thing in the situation and to direct our efforts on His behalf. This frees us from having to direct His efforts on our behalf. How liberating this is! This makes so much more sense. I have much more faith in the results of this type of prayer. Why depend on our limited wisdom and insight when we can instead depend on His?

And then there was David, "a man after God's own heart", who gave us a complete record of his prayer life, as he tended to write them down, and they became the book of Psalms. From David we learn the full extent of prayer as the communication link in our relationship with God. He records some typical request-type prayers, but most of them are just his heart-to-heart interchanges with God.

He cries out to God when he's in despair, agony or desperate. He bursts into song when his heart is full of praise, spontaneously exuding prayers of worship. He talks with God about tough situations and enemies he is facing, asking Him to help him deal with them. In deep humility and contrition, he gives us one of the best prayers of confession of sin. He seeks God's wisdom and guidance in the Word. So we see that prayer covers the complete spectrum of human relational situations, not just requests for stuff. James sums it up nicely when he says, "When you are sick or afflicted, pray. When you are happy, sing psalms." In other words, one of the secrets of prayer is to bring God into all aspects of your life, not just when you need something.

David's son, Solomon, gives us both positive and negative aspects to what his father learned about prayer. Again we see God initiating prayer when He asks Solomon to ask whatever he wants as he begins his reign over Israel. Solomon responds by praying relationally, seeking wisdom and God's guidance for the incredible task before him. Responding relationally, God gives him his request and then goes on to give him all the things he didn't ask for, as well, wealth, fame and power.

One would assume that this interchange would cement the relationship, as Solomon responds favorably to God's reaching out to him. This was not the case, however. Although God's gift of wisdom enabled Solomon to rule wisely, achieve greatness, and write most of the book of Proverbs, he wandered away from his relationship with God. His consuming interest in wealth, women and greatness led him far afield, laid the foundation for confusion in the future of his vast kingdom (2 Kings 23:13) and left him in the cynicism and regret found in Ecclesiastes. In other words, an awesome answer to prayer is of less value than a continually developing relationship with God. We would do well to take note and be instructed by this.

Daniel and his buddies provide significant insight into the secret of prayer, though not in the typical viewpoint of what prayer should do or be like. In a life or death situation, they simply ask for God's mercies to help them understand the secret, a not-so-bold approach, and God shows Daniel the secret. Faced with the burning, fiery furnace, an obvious prayer situation, there is no recorded praying, merely a very public statement of faith in God's best for them, regardless of how it turns out. God delivers them and begins His work in the heart of the king.

Under a different king and faced with death (again!) in a lion's den, Daniel sticks to his normal way of doing things. Seemingly unconcerned, he prays three times a day at his picture window, as usual, his relationship with God being the priority, not his safety. Thrown into the lion's den, there is no recorded praying, except on the part of the king, who *was* worried. Daniel spent a pleasant evening with friendly lions while the king paced his chambers. Again, God delivers Daniel, because of his relationship, not because of desperation prayers, and continues His work in the heart of the king. Apparently, good relations with God involves ordinary, everyday praying, not crisis praying. Daniel and his buddies displayed the epitome of Jesus' "not my will but Yours be done" style of surrendered life, regular prayer and relationship with God.

This brings us to Jesus in the garden, facing death. Throughout His life, Jesus demonstrated ordinary, everyday prayer, as well as extended periods of prayer to recharge His relationship with His Father. Now, in a crisis situation, Jesus does a Daniel prayer, with a little Abraham thrown in. There's a discussion of the problem, with Jesus suggesting a bypass, if possible. Then there's a submission to God's best with the resulting peace that comes from trusting His plan and power. The time involved suggests a little give and take, but the resulting confidence to face the guards indicates arrival on the same page, perfect harmony and assurance, the ultimate picture of prayer.

One more example, the apostle Paul offers further instructions along this line. Paul was a man used to instantaneous and public answers to prayer, though his first priority was his relationship with God. So when an important prayer goes unanswered, as far as he can see, he asks again, twice. Then Abraham and Daniel come into the picture again. There's some discussion with God during which Paul begins to understand the bigger picture, and then he not only surrenders to God's plan but rejoices in the accompanying infirmities, contrary to our cherished hopes for prayer, and finds peace and confidence, not a bad ending.

That's the theory, but how does it work in the real world, where things rarely go according to theory? Again, this is not a secret, not even very complicated. The key to prayer is that it is not about getting things, but rather it is the communication link in our relationship with God. And there is one foundational subsidiary thought that is often overlooked: Isn't having a relationship with God, Who is the Source of life and joy, awesome enough? What more could we really ask?

Okay, back to how it all works. Following Jesus' outline given in Matthew 6:33, we focus daily on seeking the kingdom of God and His righteousness (our relationship with Him), and everything else will take care of itself within the framework of God's guidance and provisions. For example, on the personal level, I have been following this plan for thirty-five years now. God has been gracious and faithful in His guidance and provision for me, for my family and for the ministry He gives me without any anxious, crisis-type prayers on my part. I simply do my part, and He does His, the way a true relationship should be.

We have never lacked for our needs, in spite of my amateurish money managing. God's direction has been so clear at each decision point that even I can understand. His fellowship has been intimate, encouraging and uplifting. It has been a great blessing to share life with God, but I live for the fellowship, not for the blessings.

In times of special need, there has been special provision. When, after childbirth, my wife woke up in the middle of the night hemorrhaging, I laid my hands on her and asked the Lord to stop the bleeding, and He did. This was just part of the deal, not a crisis, not a "miracle", though it would seem that way to those who need miracles.

A relationship with God is miraculous by definition, so I have come to take such occurrences as normal, not as unusual or something to be constantly sought after. Providing just what we need just when we need it is so God-like, why should I be surprised? When prayer is not about getting things, there is such freedom in knowing God and sharing each day with Him.

So how does all this theory about prayer really work when your son is a Marine in a combat zone? This is where the rubber hits the road, where theory becomes critical reality. How are you supposed to pray? What should you expect in prayer? How should you react to God if your son is killed? Has prayer failed? Has God failed you?

Let's start at the beginning, applying the principles we have discussed. First there was the faithful, continually developing relationship with God. This provided a stable basis for life, for prayer and for ministry to our son. As a result of prayer and the priorities in our growing relationship with the Lord, we were privileged to lead him to Christ at the age of three, the beginning of his own developing relationship with God. Through the years, we continued in faithful relationship with the Lord, which included sharing with our son the things of Jesus and the Word, prayer for him daily and surrendering him to the Lord daily, as we did ourselves. As a result, we had the joy of watching the development of his steady relationship with the Lord, which was a blessing to him, to us, and to those around him as he grew to be a strong Christian man.

"Wait a minute," you say, "What does this have to do with praying for a soldier in a dangerous combat zone in Iraq?"

This has everything to do with that. Remember our prayer principles. Prayer is simply the communication link in our relationship with God, not about getting things. With that relationship as the foundation, we all were now ready for his deployment to Iraq, confident in God's plan, power and provision for all our needs. We prayed for grace, guidance and strength for him every day. All of us surrendered his life constantly into God's care and service. We prayed for him, talked to him often and were proud of his service for the Lord, his country and for the Iraqi people.

He was killed in action in the week before the first Iraqi elections. His story was on the front page right beside a picture of an Iraqi woman voting for the first time in her life. A thousand people came to his funeral and heard at least five clear presentations of the Gospel, as that which was the closest to Jesse's heart was shared again and again. The story of his faith went out on international wire services and internet links around the world. We heard just a fraction of the stories about the lives that were touched, and those were incredible and are still coming in. Surrendered to the Lord, the Lord used him in a mighty way. What greater fulfillment could you ask for?

But what about Mom and Dad and their prayers? As parents, we pray for good and worthwhile lives for our children. Jesse had a wonderful and truly worthwhile life whose impact will continue for years to come. As a father, I take my responsibility seriously for getting my children safely home, and I work and pray to that end. Though it was sooner rather than later and not exactly the way I had in mind, with God's help, I saw Jesse get safely home. And God has carried and comforted and used us in our times of deepest grief. In the context of surrendered lives, our prayers were answered beyond our wildest dreams.

While we're on the subject, let me share with you our experience with prayer in relation to Jesse's burial service. This was scheduled for Memorial Day in the afternoon, following the morning community memorial observances, and people were coming from all over the country to share the day and the services with us. We had been praying for good weather for the service and for all the traveling, but it had been dark and rainy for ten days and was supposed to be the same for Memorial Day. It was going to take a miracle for the sun to break through.

As we drove to the morning observances under a dark and threatening sky, I realized that we had been praying improperly. I told my wife that we needed to be praying for perfect weather, not for good weather. Following our prayer principles, we should be seeking His plan, since He knew what weather would be best for all that needed to be accomplished in every dimension of that day. As always, that thought brought to my heart peace and even joy concerning the day's weather. Here's what the Lord did so perfectly with the day.

There were only sprinkles during the parade, in which Jesse's Marines marched smartly in their dress blues. During the dedication of a memorial site that followed, it began to rain. Everyone put up their umbrellas while the Marines stood at attention in the rain, an awe inspiring sight in those circumstances. My daughter summed it up best when she said that it would not have seemed right to be sunny, bright and cheerful during that solemn occasion. The large crowd seemed totally undeterred by the weather. There were heartfelt observations that the rain served to add to the significance of the situation, as well as binding us all together in remembrance. Several people remarked on the appropriateness of my invocation, in which I thanked the Lord for weeping with us, which is truly how it felt. We drove home through showers to prepare for the afternoon burial.

The rain let up for the transfer of the casket to the hearse, but as we followed it up to the hilltop cemetery, it seemed like we were going back into a dark cloud. Thunder rolled in the distance, which seemed to bring the solemnity of God's presence close again. When the service began with the Marine pallbearers carrying the casket to its final resting place, we experienced what the reporter on the scene aptly called "a brief splash of sunshine on an otherwise rain-soaked day". The birdsong-filled sunlight bathed the scene like a special benediction as we shared the joy of the living hope of the resurrection and told him we'd see him soon. It was perfect weather and an incredible moment.

When the service was over, God began to weep again, and the thunder sounded like sorrowful groaning as people got back to their cars. We all filed down to our house for some time together with a little food. We had a large tent in the back yard, so the rain was not a problem at all.

It was a properly somber Memorial Day/burial day. The weather was not good, but rather perfect, with rain and sun coming at the most appropriate times to complete the atmosphere of that hallowed day, a day to treasure in our memories for the rest of our lives. It was truly a day planned in exquisite detail by the Lord for all of us that were involved. Several expressed agreement with a Marine who left his family in Texas to come all the way to Vermont to share Memorial Day with us, "I couldn't think of a more fitting way to mark this year's Memorial Day."

This experience reminds me of another prayer principle Paul shares with us in the eighth chapter of Romans, "Likewise the Spirit also helps our infirmities; for we know not what we should pray for as we ought: but the Spirit Himself makes intercession for us with groanings which cannot be uttered. And He that searches the hearts knows what is the mind of the Spirit, because He makes intercession for the saints according to the will of God." Again in the context of surrendered lives, as we bring our needs to the Lord in our helplessness, the Spirit adjusts our prayers according to the will of God, Who so often responds beyond what we can ask or think. For me, this is a far deeper experience of the power and grace of God than just getting what I wanted.

So, what have we learned about the secret of prayer? First of all, that there is no secret, because God offers Himself freely to all who come to Him with all their heart. Then we see that prayer is not about getting things, but rather is the communication link in our relationship with God. Finally, the key to prayer is a surrendered life that involves regular prayer and rest in God's plan, love and power that results in a lack of need for crisis prayers. Whew! I got a lot out of that. I hope you did, too.

References: - God's heart: Deut.5:29, Rom.8:32, Matt.6:33, John 15:7 - Enoch: Gen.5:24 - Abraham: James 2:23, Gen.18 - Moses: Ex.32 - Joshua: Jos.5:13-15- Solomon: 1 Kings 3 - Daniel: Dan.2, 3, 6 - Paul: 2 Cor.12:7-10

A prayer corollary

It's not whether God can do it; or if we can get God to do it, but if we can follow in faith – Joshua 4:20-24.

Chapter six

Pastoring: Purpose, Authority, Responsibility

JESUS WAS THE BEST PASTOR who ever lived and shared in ministry. Because He was so many other wonderful, significant things, we often overlook this facet of His example to us. As we examine His ministry from this perspective, we learn some great things about pastoring.

Purpose

Throughout the Old Testament and into Jesus' ministry, one basic concept emerges in relation to our present consideration – people (sheep) need a shepherd (pastor). Isaiah summed it up by saying, "All we like sheep have gone astray..." and Jesus addressed His purpose by saying, "I have come to seek and to save that which was lost." This is the purpose of pastoring, shepherding the church. Jesus calls Himself the Good Shepherd, and the New Testament often refers to pastors in these terms. It's simply a fact of life that people need good leadership. The church is no different, and that is the purpose of pastors.

Pondered from this perspective, the basic purpose of pastoring is more easily understood. A pastor is to use his God-given gifts and talents for the purpose of leading, edifying and caring for the people under his care. This does not mean pampering people or doing everything for them. Jesus never did that, even when He could have done so simply by saying the word. Instead, He was working on helping people grow toward maturity in their lives, in their relationship with God and in their own ministry. According to Him, this is what it meant to be a good shepherd.

Jesus used all His abilities, wisdom and power as a Shepherd to accomplish this purpose, and His example should move us in that direction, as well. People need that kind of leadership, from Jesus and from pastors. A pastor's primary purpose is to care for his people and to lead them toward maturity, and a proper focus on this purpose will lead to a healthy pastorate and a healthy church.

Authority

This is a problem area in pastoring, for the simple reason that we are all human beings affected by the fall, which makes it difficult to follow Christ's example without human motives and impulses interfering. However, if we examine His example, we will have a better chance of being able to follow it. So, let's look at His authority and how He used it.

Jesus was sent from God with all the gifts and abilities He needed to do His job well, and God gave Him the authority to use them to accomplish His purpose. This translates into the area of pastoring in a fairly straightforward way. We want a pastor who has been sent by God, with all the gifts and abilities needed to do his job well, but then we want to tell him how to use them, rather than giving him the authority associated with his abilities. This actually hinders the pastor's best use of his gifts and talents and works against what we hired him to do; not the wisest use of a pastor.

We have a propensity to fall into that trap because, though Jesus used His authority for our good, rather than for His personal profit, human pastors sometimes have different tendencies. Perhaps the wisest route is somewhere in the middle. We should give pastors authority to do what we hired them for, unless they prove themselves unworthy of that trust, at which point we need to re-evaluate, reassess and rework our arrangement with them, hopefully growing together into what the Lord has for the church. In the meantime, we should constantly keep in mind that we all, pastor and people, are under the authority of Jesus, the Head of the church, and we will each give account to Him.

Responsibility

With the purpose of caring for the people and leading them toward maturity, pastors have the responsibility to teach and do those things which would move their flock in that direction. Jesus employed the strategy of a player/coach to accomplish this purpose.

He coached them through sermons, direct instructions and by giving assignments and answering questions. He demonstrated what He was saying by being a "player" Himself, doing all the things He was telling them to do and more. These are good guidelines for a pastor's responsibility, as well.

A pastor has the responsibility of painstaking preaching, in order to give his people the Bible information they need for a foundation for life and growth. Pastors should also offer personal instructions to fit the individual needs of those who come with questions. Pastors should also give challenges and "assignments"; so people have a means of trying out what they are learning, ideally with the pastor beside them the first few times to clarify and encourage. And finally, people should be able to see the pastor demonstrating, in his own personal life and ministry, the things being taught; so they can see how they work and how they apply in everyday life.

As to specific responsibilities, they will become obvious as the above guidelines are applied with an eye to including others in ministry, which contributes to their growth. For example, a pastor should visit the sick, while encouraging and teaching others how to do so, as well. The pastor should be reaching out to his community, while encouraging and teaching others how to do so, as well. A pastor should be developing good preaching skills, while encouraging and teaching others how to do so, as well. A pastor should be looking out for the well being of the people in his care, while encouraging and teaching others how to do so, as well.

In this way, the player/coach strategy Jesus exemplified can be fulfilled in pastoral ministry.

Another critical responsibility which falls under the good shepherd design of pastoring exemplified by Jesus is that of protecting the flock. When the soldiers came to arrest Him in the garden, He identified Himself as the One they were looking for and asked them to let the others go. He had already warned the disciples that this was going to happen, in order to protect them when it did. Besides the physical protection He offered here, He also warned them of other problems they would face, in order to protect them from psychological damage when those problems appeared.

In the same way, as the pastor has the experience and overview wisdom to see problems, he has the responsibility to take steps to protect the flock when those problems arise, physical, psychological or spiritual. There are "wolves" out there, and part of the pastor's responsibility is to warn the flock and, if need be, make the decisions and take steps to personally shield and safeguard the flock. This is part of the attitude a person must have in order to qualify as a good pastor, as Jesus outlined in John 10, where He says a good shepherd will interpose himself between the flock and the wolf, while a poor one will run away.

Now, I realize that in the modern church the pastor is expected to carry many other responsibilities, from printing up the bulletins to running the building program. However, these responsibilities could be handled by non-pastors, which would free up the pastor to fulfill his responsibility of caring for the people and leading them toward maturity. The pastor can only work best if the people work with him, doing their part. In this way, all the responsibilities are met by the people best suited to handle them, and the church becomes what it was meant to be without overload on any one person.

A proper perspective on pastoring will result in blessing for the pastor. It will result in blessing for the people in the church. It will result in blessing for Jesus, as He longs for His people and His church to grow toward maturity. And it will result in blessing for the community and the world, which longs to see a church characterized by the love and leadership of Jesus.

May God bless you pastors and your people as you work together within the design and example which Jesus laid out for you.

Chapter seven

Gospel/Salvation, Apologetics and Evangelism

THIS IS WHERE JESSE'S HEART was. He loved Jesus and loved to share with others the redemption he had found in Him. He went to seminary for the express purpose of preparing himself to be able to share the Gospel better. This is what motivated him, what moved him the most, the desire to share with others the joy he had found in Jesus.

As far as Jesse was concerned, everything else in life was secondary to this and should be made to serve this main purpose. If he had the opportunity to speak, he used it to share, as simply and clearly as he could, how you could find a personal relationship with Jesus, the Savior. One of our few remaining recordings of his voice is of a speech he gave in his college dorm, in which he used several simple illustrations to clarify the Gospel message, with the purpose of making it more accessible to his hearers. He would have been pleased to know that that recording was featured in a TV special documentary about the incident in which he died, pleased to know that it might have helped point someone else to the Savior he loved.

His Marine staff sergeant likes to say that Jesse could pick up a stick off the ground and use it to illustrate the Gospel in such a way as to make it more understandable. He was always talking with his fellow Marines, including his commanding officers, about the things of the Lord, though not in an obnoxious way. It was just an integral part of who he was, and his buddies appreciated who he was enough to appoint him honorary chaplain of the platoon and asked him to pray before each mission, including his final one. One of his buddies told us, "I've never felt safer than right after Jesse prayed", although it was a safety in the Lord that Jesse craved, not necessarily physical safety.

Therefore, in asking me to write this chapter, Jesse was asking me to write about something that he already knew a lot about. In typical Jesse fashion, he just wanted to get a little more insight that might help him do a better job. So here, out of years of Bible study about and experience in sharing the Gospel, I put down a few things I've learned. I hope it helps you to do a better job of sharing what Jesse knew was the most important message in the world.

Getting to know God

What an awesome, almost unbelievable, concept, that the finite, seemingly insignificant, beings that we are can actually enter into an intimate personal relationship with the infinite and infinitely significant

Being Who is the Creator of the universe! Even more amazing is the fact that He is willing to be known. But the most extraordinary part of the concept is that He has paid an incredible price to make it possible to know Him. Let's examine the elements of this awesome concept.

To begin with, it's important to understand that God is a person Who can be known just as we can know any person. We were created in His image partly for the purpose of being able to relate to Him. We can communicate with Him. We can at least begin to understand Him and what He is like. We can begin to know how He feels about things, what makes Him happy, what makes Him sad. We can get a glimpse of His heart and the things that are important to Him. He is a person Who can be known, and He is willing to be known. Incredible!

In the Garden of Eden, God came in the cool of the evening to spend time with Adam and Eve, to talk with them, to share with them, to care for them, to let them and us know that He was willing to be known. After thousands of years of people wandering away from Him, He reminded us, through the prophet Jeremiah, that He was still willing, still accessible to anyone who would seek Him with all their heart. And then, in His most powerful expression of willingness to be known, He sent Jesus to open the door for reconciliation for anyone who would come. He is willing. The only question is, are we?

Since He is willing, even desirous to have us get to know Him, He has provided several ways for us to do that. First, He reveals Himself to us through His Word. In His Word He reveals, not just descriptions of Himself, but His heart and mind, as well. In the Ten Commandments, for example, we think He is just laying out the rules for us to follow, so we'll "behave ourselves." But what He is really showing us is how He feels about things, what's important to Him, valuable insights we would need to get to know anyone. In what we ordinarily call "the love chapter", He's not just telling us what love is supposed to be like. He is also revealing what His heart is like, how He acts and reacts, an extremely intimate self portrait that we rarely get from another person, yet He freely discloses it to us. In the description of the "fruit of the Spirit" He reveals His nature and character in a way that we seldom are allowed to see by even close friends. And then, as we watch Him act and react in numerous situations throughout history, much of the rest of what we need to know about Him is revealed, so that we can approach Him and get to know Him with confidence.

We spend hours in conversation to get to know people. We ought to come to God's Word with the same depth of desire, literally "hungering and thirsting" for intimacy with the most wonderful Person in the universe. He makes Himself readily available through His Word. Don't waste that opportunity.

The second way He has provided for us to get to know Him is through His Son, Jesus Christ, in Whom is "all the fullness of the Godhead bodily." Jesus repeatedly told His disciples that if they had seen Him they had seen the Father. And Jesus reiterates God's invitation to get to know Him. He states that He even stands at our door and knocks, encouraging us to invite Him in to share a meal and fellowship with Him. How much more available can anyone make himself?

This brings us to the third way God has provided for us to get to know Him, by personally spending time with Him as He has spent time with people down through the millenniums. Enoch had such close companionship with God that He took him home early. Abraham came to be known as the friend of God. David filled Psalm after Psalm with fellowship with God in all kinds of situations. Anna spent more than fifty years in prayer in the temple and wound up being one of the first to see and hold the Savior when He came. Paul was willing to share in the "fellowship of His sufferings" to know Him better and felt like He was making progress. Down through the years people have gotten to know God by just spending time with Him.

We have the same kind of opportunities, if we'll take advantage of them. The invitation to come to Him is still open. We can read the Bible daily. Jesus still knocks at the door of our hearts. God is still available to walk with us in the cool of the evening or anytime. We can talk with Him in prayer in any situation, under any conditions. Are you getting to know Him today?

References - God is a Person: Gen.1:26-27, 5:1 - willing to be known: Gen.3:8-9, Jer.29:13, 2 Cor.5:18-19 - known through Scriptures: Ex.20:1-17, Eph.4:24-5:2, 1 Cor.13:4-7, Gal.5:22-23 - thirsting for God: Psalm 42:1-2 - known through Jesus: John 10:38, 14:9, Col.2:9,

Thoughts for Jesse

Rev.3:20 - known through fellowship: Gen.5:22-24, James 2:23, Psalm 23 & 51, Phil.3:7-12 - aspiration: Rev.3:20, Col.2:6-7

God introduces Himself to us

We were created to share life with God, so, when Adam and Eve moved away from Him, and we have each in our turn followed suit, a monkey wrench was thrown into the works that messes up everything, as explained earlier. However, rather than just saying, "They deserve what they get", which He could have done, God took pity on us, planning the means of redemption from before the beginning. And, in the same way as He came seeking Adam and Eve after the fall, He comes seeking each of us.

He comes gently, however, not blasting into our lives as He certainly could. Knowing that we are slow to understand and to believe, He doesn't hurry us or coerce us. Instead, He introduces Himself tenderly along lines that we can relate to, giving us time to understand and respond in a personal way. Jesus and the way He walked among us is the perfect example of this.

He came softly, unobtrusively, as a baby, giving the world about thirty years to get used to the idea of "God with us". Then He walked among us gently, teaching, listening, helping, healing, with an occasional challenge to help us deal with and respond to the truth. He called twelve to "follow Him", to watch, listen, learn

78

and participate, so they could decide for themselves, with full understanding, whether or not they wanted to make a lifelong commitment to faith. One of the twelve decided not to continue. Another flunked the final exam before going on to lead the church. All had the opportunity to see Jesus completely before deciding; because that's the way He is, for them and for us.

Don Richardson, in <u>Peace Child</u>, speaks of how God builds a key into each culture that enables people to understand redemption in their own terms so they can respond. He shared a powerful illustration of how God prepared a jungle tribe to understand redemption, how God had introduced Himself to them. Having personally experienced this over and over, consider these examples.

When I was a boy, my mother told me about God, and I went to Sunday school regularly, but I had no personal experience with Him until one cold, winter day as I was walking home from school. Between school and home there was a wide open flat where the winter wind was torturous ordinarily. That day it was blowing so hard that snow filled the air, and I couldn't even see the other side. It had been one of those days, and this seemed more than I could bear.

In child-like faith I petitioned the Lord, something I'd never done before at that spot, "If you could hold the wind for a minute, I'd appreciate it. I'll run as fast as I can." I took off as fast as I could go, and the wind was calm the whole way across. When I had reached the shelter of the trees on the other side, I turned and looked back. The wind and snow were blowing as wildly as before. Though it was several more years before I understood and responded to God's invitation to eternal life through Jesus, His precious Son, He took the time to introduce Himself to me that day in a way that I could fully appreciate. Perhaps that was why I responded so readily to His invitation when it came.

Another time, I was sharing the Gospel with a young woman, and used Paul's analogy of adoption to explain how God wanted us to become His children. I told her that God had already drawn up the adoption papers and only required her consent to finalize the process of making her His own child. After she prayed to receive Christ, she shared that she had been adopted as a child, God's preparation for her coming to Himself.

A friend was sharing Christ with an older woman one day, and, having reached an impasse, called me. She said the woman had always believed in Jesus, had received answers to prayer, but had never made a personal commitment to the Savior. What advice could I give that would help her understand what she needed to do? The answer seemed obvious to me – Jesus had been introducing Himself to the woman, wooing her for years, and now was proposing. She simply had to respond with a "yes" or "no". My friend shared that thought with the woman, who subsequently said "yes" to Jesus as her Savior.

God is seeking us, inviting us to come home to Him and the incredible life He has for us. He initiates the process, introducing Himself to us in ways we can readily understand. It is ours but to respond for the reconciliation to be completed, for the life-giving relationship to be restored.

Obtaining mercy and finding grace

As I was studying the concept of Christ as our high priest, I arrived at an interesting conclusion, which though directly related to that concept, is a powerful and important concept of its own – ultimately we are each responsible for our own lives. Life is a gift from God to each of us individually, and we are responsible for what we do with it. It is vital to consider why this is an important concept.

This idea seems obvious at first, and we revel in the thought that we are the master of our destinies... on the surface. However, sooner or later, we begin to labor under that responsibility and seek to escape it, mainly in the form of excuses. Making excuses for our behavior has become a national sport in our culture, elevated to its highest level by our obsession with the psychoanalytical approach to almost everything. We are not responsible because... "my father was an alcoholic"; "my mother spanked me" or "my mother didn't spank me enough"; "I grew up on the wrong side of the tracks"; etc., etc.

If we become a Christian, we add another dimension to our seeking to escape from responsibility, and whole branches of theology have developed devoted exclusively to this pursuit. "Deliverance" is a favorite, as we seek to make God responsible for setting us free from our sinful tendencies. There are several different approaches to trying to make God responsible for "fixing" us, so that we won't misbehave any longer. With all the power of God available, we want Him to be responsible for that, rather than taking any responsibility ourselves.

However, the Bible clearly and repeatedly states that we are each individually, personally responsible for our own lives, and we will ultimately answer to God for what we do with them. When we stand at judgment, we will never hear or say, "My father was an alcoholic, etc., etc." Excuses go out the window, and all those who were counting on their practiced excuses will stand silent before God. So how does all this relate to the concept of Christ as our high priest? What is He willing to do for us? He is willing to help us, as we fulfill our responsibilities for our own lives.

We cannot expect Him to do it for us, because, as we've pointed out earlier, He gives us life as a gift to do with as we wish. That's part of the fun. However, when we are ready to do our part, taking the responsibility, He is ready to help us, teach us, hold us, strengthen us, guide us, and show us the way. Let's look at a few passages which outline what He is willing to do for us, while we do our part.

Isaiah 41:10 says, "Fear not; for I am with you: be not dismayed; for I am your God: I will strengthen you; I will help you; I will uphold you with the right hand of my righteousness." With all His declaration of strength and help here, He never says He will do it for us.

He says He will help us do that which is our responsibility to do; so we need not be afraid. We can face each day and every situation knowing He is by our side, doing His part while we do ours.

Ephesians 3:16 is a prayer which includes the thought, "...that He would grant you, according to the riches of His glory, to be strengthened with might by His Spirit in the inner man..."Here we see a reference to His glory and His Spirit ready, not to do it for us, but to strengthen us from the inside out as we seek to fulfill our responsibility. This is a reminder of our need for help to do our part, as well as a guide for how to pray for those in need, not a way out of our responsibility. This also removes weakness as an excuse.

Colossians 1:11-12a is the worst one, adding a request for patience and longsuffering to the prayer that we may be "...strengthened with all might, according to His glorious power, unto all patience and longsuffering with joyfulness; giving thanks unto the Father..." And what's with this longsuffering with joyfulness stuff? Are we supposed to be joyful when things take longer than we had hoped? Are we supposed to keep plugging along with our part until our responsibility is complete? Apparently so, as He applies His glorious power to strengthen us with all the might we will need to carry on. Not only are all excuses removed, but also any hope of rights to complain or to be impatient and grumpy.

The obvious conclusion is that our High Priest will not use His glory, His power or His Spirit to do things for us, but He will help and strengthen us as we fulfill our responsibility. He wants us to share in the labor so we can share in the reward. He wants us to grow strong and fulfilled as we conquer increasingly difficult tasks with His help and strength to support us.

Reconciliation (Salvation)

If our relationship with God was broken at the fall of Adam and Eve, what bridges the gap so that we can begin to know God again? This is the underlying problem that must be solved within the idea of reconciliation. Ordinarily, we think that we must somehow do something or be something in order to reach God. However, salvation is not possible unless God makes provision for reconciliation, which, thankfully, He has.

We have a tendency to underestimate the plan of God and His determination to carry it out. He created a world designed to share with Him for eternity. When we disrupted that plan by choosing our own plan, which ran counter to His, He simply moved to plan B, which, if you consider that He knew He was going to need it, perhaps was just the second part of the original plan. Built into plan A was the way for us to find our way home after we had wandered away and gotten lost. For God's original plan to see fulfillment, He had to include a provision for reconciliation.

This provision includes the death and resurrection of Jesus as a means of paying the penalty of sin; so God could be "just and the Justifier of all who came to Him through Christ", "the Way, the Truth and the Life". It also includes the encouraging power of His Spirit, Who draws us out of the dark, comfortable swamp of sin into the more attractive light and freedom of forgiveness and fellowship with God, if we will respond in a positive way to His call. It also includes bringing people around us who can explain it in such a way that we can understand and know how we need to respond, as I explain in the personal experience section of the chapter on Theology.

All of this works together to extend to us God's gracious offer of reconciliation. Reconciliation or salvation is God attempting to reach us, because the gap is too great and we are too weak to reach the other way. Our part of the process is to simply take the rescuing hand extended to us, to say "Yes!" to His offer.

There are entire volumes written on all the details of salvation, but they all boil down to the simple description written here. I am thankful for that, because I could understand it well enough to receive it and begin my journey with the Savior while understanding it more and more as time goes on. Even a child can grasp the simple elements of salvation and say "Yes!" to Jesus. In fact, Jesus said we must all receive it as a child, lest we complicate it and miss the point completely, thinking there is something we must add to make it work.

The Bible says salvation is a gift offered freely to all who will receive it from the heart. God offers reconciliation in this way, because any other way would be beyond our capability, and He wants us to be able to find our way home. I am so thankful for His amazing grace which made it simple enough for me to understand. May God bless you as you receive and enjoy the simplicity of reconciliation, as well.

The postmodern era

I just returned from a pastor's conference in which they were discussing ways to accomplish ministry in the postmodern era, apparently the time period in which we find ourselves. Now, I understand that historians, sociologists and anthropologists need to label time periods to help us understand the flow of history and its various components, such as early times, medieval times, the industrial revolution, modern times, etc., but postmodern? This terminology is such a downer, as though it's all over, the far side of the hill, it's all down hill from here. The other names were more optimistic, neutral at the worst, but not negative. Why not "the technological revolution", "the global information age", or something equally descriptive of a change of eras, without being negative?

I have come to the conclusion that "they" like the term postmodern era because it has an ominous sound to it, almost an end of the world type of feel to it. It is as though it is the latest of the ongoing challenges to human survival, like the nuclear age or the ice age. The result is an increased feeling of importance, of "what do we need to do to deal with this challenge?" type of thinking. And the church sees a new set of cultural circumstances to overcome or adapt to in order to continue in successful ministry, a new challenge to be relevant, which brings us to the point.

Jesus and God's truth is already and always relevant. They need no repackaging in order to be palatable to a new generation or culture. When the real Gospel is shared by real people with the real love of God in real settings, it is always relevant and life-changing for anyone who is truly interested and responds from the heart. That was Jesus' plan when He walked among us and remains His plan for His disciples as they carry on His ministry in a troubled world in which the needs of the human heart do not change, no matter how the culture changes.

Approach and delivery

Every concerned Christian, who wants to share the precious message of the Savior with others, initially has questions about how to approach people with the Gospel and how to present it most effectively. They often think there must be some secret involved, especially when their initial attempts meet with mixed results – exuberant preaching resulting in fairly dramatic negative responses. Then they begin to settle down and want to learn the "secret".

The secret is actually very simple. The Holy Spirit is constantly at work in the world, drawing people to

Jesus, and He needs us to be a witness people can see and hear and question, in order to understand things from a human perspective. Therefore, if we begin with an attitude of surrender, ready to be involved in the process, the Lord can plug us in at His convenience, in His timing and location. One of my greatest blessings has been to watch that work and be part of God's working in someone else's redemption.

The next question is delivery, often stated something like, "How do you bring the conversation around to the subject of salvation?" I have found that this is **not** really the right question. In my experience, if you are in an attitude of surrender for God's use, you can start any way you want, and He will use it to accomplish His purpose. Therefore the real question is "Are you fully surrendered for His use at this moment?" If you are, God can and will use you to help others, no matter how you begin.

I was traveling on a bus and had been praying for an opportunity to share the Gospel with someone (the attitude of surrender), when a young man sat down beside me and began to visit. After a while, I just blurted out what was probably a dumb opening gambit in my desire to share the Gospel, but God used it to accomplish His purpose, because I was at least willing to try to fit into His plan.

I asked, "Have you ever heard about Jesus?" Not particularly creative or evocative, according to evangelism seminars, but in God's hands, it worked. The young man replied, "Yes, I have, but I'd like to hear what you have to say about it." And I got to share the Gospel with a willing listener.

I have found that if, out of a love for Him and for others, you are willing to have the Lord use you, you can begin just about any way, and as soon as you mention the name of Jesus, the Holy Spirit takes it from there. So the delivery is not so much about the words we say or the method we use, as it is about a sweet spirit offered in surrender to the Lord for His use. He's ready to go when we are.

One important key

One thing which I have found to be the key to success in witnessing is to make sure you are sharing the Gospel out of love, rather than because you want to straighten someone out. The latter approach turns people off, as it comes across as being judgmental. Love opens doors, as it communicates concern for people's best interest and offers solutions, rather than put downs.

Chapter eight

Parenting

WE HAD SUCH A GOOD time as a family when Jesse was growing up that he asked me to include a section on parenting, even though, or perhaps because, I never read any parenting book besides the Bible. He wanted me to put into writing my thoughts on parenting, so he would have them as a resource for his own family. That will never happen now; so it hardly seems necessary for me to write this. However, there is now another factor for me to consider.

A young mother sent her condolences after Jesse died, and we automatically sent her a copy of "New Normal" and directed her to the Jesse website. She wrote back to say that they had made radical changes in their lives to spend more time with their children, as I had implored parents to do in "New Normal", and she asked me to send some parenting tips. I told her I didn't really do that, but there was going to be a section on parenting in the book Jesse asked me to write. She said she looked forward to reading it.

So, Julianna, this is from Jesse's dad to you and all young mothers and fathers who desire to raise wonderful children to bless the world around them. May God bless you as you set out to do that. May you find the same joy that we knew in enjoying Jesse. There are so many factors and situations involved in parenting that I will not attempt to cover them all but will address three basic concepts which give the foundation for good parenting.

The first one is profound in its simplicity and in its far reaching effect – good parenting comes out of a good relationship with your heavenly Father. Before you can even begin to commit yourself to good parenting, you must commit yourself to doing whatever it takes to develop a good relationship with God. God is the best example of good parenting, and as you allow Him to transform you by the renewing of your mind (Romans 12:1-2), you will be best equipped to raise your children properly. With His example, His thoughts and His heart to guide you, you will be able to help your children find the path of life and joy (Psalm 16:11). And you will find one of the greatest joys in this life, that of sharing fellowship with God with your children in everyday life.

It was who we were, not just something that we did, which made parenting work. The result was that every part of our lives became teachable moments to share a little something about the Lord with our children (Deuteronomy 6:6-7). Because our lives were focused on our relationship with the Lord, we were able to pass that priority on to our children. They grew up with a desire to please Him, not just to please us, and that desire transformed their lives. When they understood that we were in that together, that made parenting so much easier, and we grew close as we grew closer to the Lord together.

The second concept is profound in its practicality and in its strategic impact – say what you mean, and mean what you say. We have all witnessed scenes in the store of kids begging for things, their parents saying "No!" and then getting it for them after all. It is more than obvious what that teaches the kids – the parent doesn't really mean what they say.

What is not so obvious is the underlying lesson for the children – I can't trust what my parent says. This is the basis for growing insecurity for the child and for increased testing to find out if there is some point at which they can begin to trust what their parent says. They will push until they find that point, because children long for security, security which only their parents can provide. The key in this is for the parent to provide that point as soon as possible. The testing, and the resulting conflict, will stop when the child feels secure, knowing they can trust what their parents say.

This is actually very simple, especially in the early stages. Be careful what you promise or what you threaten. Always think about what you are telling your children, with an eye to whether or not you mean it and whether or not you can follow through on what you say. This is critical! Your children's security, sense of well being, and their corresponding behavior depend upon it.

And then always, no matter what, always follow through. Otherwise, your children will not believe you, and your relationship with them will begin to crumble, along with their security. If you threaten a punishment, then punish them. If you promise a reward, then reward them. Let them see, not just hear, that you mean what you say.

I have said this is simple in the early stages, because it is extremely difficult to remedy later. I have had so many parents tell me they are struggling to build a relationship with their teenagers. Of course they are! They should have built that relationship years ago; so it would be a normal part of their lives, ready to face together the teenage years. All I can say at this point is that the parent must begin with an apology for wasting all those years, and seek the teenager's help in remedying the relationship situation. The love demonstrated by such an apology may be enough to begin to bridge the gap.

Say what you mean, and mean what you say. That's it in a nutshell. If you will do that you will build a good foundation for good parenting, as well as building a solid foundation for your children's security and good behavior.

The third is profound in its effect on your attitude and theirs – enjoy your children. This affects your attitude toward your children, how you view them and the challenges of parenting. It also really affects their attitude toward you, as they immediately pick up on how you feel about them. They know intuitively whether you think they are a burden or a blessing, and they will act and react accordingly.

Early in our parenting experience, we encountered over and over again parents who couldn't seem to wait to get a vacation from their children. They would say, in front of their children, "We're farming our kids out this weekend, so we can get away for a break." A break from your kids? What does that tell your children?

We decided we would never, ever use that kind of terminology, whether our children were there or not, because we never felt that way. We wanted them to know that we liked being with them, that we thought it was fun to be with them, that they were a joy and a blessing in our lives. What do you think that told our children?

When you bring children into the world, they must become your priority. That's what it means to be a parent. Children are not just an accident, a footnote, a fringe benefit to marriage. Children are the priority. Right now! Not later, when it's convenient or when it fits with your career. If you don't want your children, put them up for adoption. Don't just farm them out or ignore them or let someone else raise them. The most precious time you have with your children is *now*. Any other attitude communicates with them that you don't really like them, and you should not be surprised to discover that they don't really like you.

Now, I'm not talking about acting like your children are the center of the world. To artificially elevate them in that way sets them up for a drastic fall when they are faced with the reality of an uncaring world. Your children are probably not much more special than all the other children in the world, and they need to understand that so they can honestly find their place. They just need to know that they are special to you, and they need to experience that in how you act and react around them.

We enjoyed every moment with our children. We adjusted our careers to allow us to do that (It can be done!). We took them everywhere it was appropriate to take children and adjusted our schedules to have one of us home with them when it wasn't appropriate to take them with us. We only got babysitters when it was absolutely necessary, and sometimes we didn't even then, as in the following example.

In order to build up the dulcimer business I was doing, we gave concerts to introduce people to the dulcimer, with me playing the dulcimer and my wife accompanying me on the guitar. The first couple of times we got a babysitter, so we could focus on the concert. Then I had a different idea, as I was always seeking ways to have the kids be with us. I told them I would pay them what I paid a babysitter if they would go with us and baby sit themselves. In other words they would have to quietly behave themselves during the concert, and we could share the drive and the rest of the evening together. This was when all three were less than ten years old.

You might think this sounded like a recipe for disaster; turning three young children lose to fend for themselves during an important business event. It turned out to be one of my best ideas, as far as both they and we were concerned. They knew exactly what was expected of them and had strong motivation to do it – they wanted to get paid. They sat on the edge of the room or in the next room and occupied themselves quietly, reading or coloring or whatever quiet activity they chose. It worked out extremely well, and our children realized again that we enjoyed them and loved to have them with us.

They had to listen to our little concert over and over (they have my jokes and patter all memorized, even now), but this situation gave us more time together, sharing experiences, treats afterward, and our lives in its many facets. They were very well behaved, usually drawing questions from the crowd about how we made them do that. The crowd laughed when I answered that we paid them, but the kids knew that we just loved to have them with us.

And that's the way it was whenever we could manage it. We enjoyed them, and they didn't seem to mind having us around. The transition to the teen years was a smooth one, because the relationship was strong to start with, and though they tried to help us keep up with the latest music, fashions and technology, they were never embarrassed to be with us in public.

When Jesse needed another man to fill out his bowling league, he asked me. When I needed someone to go golfing with me, I asked Jesse. This relationship style continues to this day. When we decided to travel out west this summer, we all went together – Mom and Dad and a thirty-year-old and a twenty-six-year-old – and we found that we still enjoy each other. What a blessing it has been all these years, and it all began when we set out to intentionally enjoy our children.

So, enjoy your children. Arrange your schedule (and your career, if need be) to make them your priority. Share each stage of their lives. Don't miss a moment, if you can help it. You'll never regret it, and you'll be blessed, as we were, with the joy that God intended children to be. And if one passes on before you, as Jesse did, you can face even that knowing that you have no unfinished business, which is an amazing foundation for surviving the grief.

So that's it. I realize that there are many specific question areas that I could address. But, if you will focus on these three basic concepts, you'll have the foundation you need for figuring out for yourself the answers to the rest of the specific, personal questions you will face. Part of the joy of parenting is to explore that world with your children with the Lord's help and guidance. May God bless you as you do that.

Hope for the next generation

2 Chronicles 29 tells us that no matter the sins of the fathers, the next generation can make good choices, have a right relationship with God and have a good life. I am so thankful that, through the Lord's grace and help, the cycle of dysfunction can be broken, and you can have a good life and pass it on to your children. So, do it, for your children's sake, as well as for your own sake. Learn from the mistakes of others. Don't make them all yourself.

"Jesse always had style."

"Jesse (center) with brother Matthew and sister Heather"

"Jesse with Grandpa"

"Jesse flying at the beach"

"Jesse's high-school senior picture"

"Jesse and Dad after finishing second
in the state championship game"

"Jesse and Mom at boot camp graduation"

"Jesse loved his snacks"

"Jesse with Mom and Dad"

"Jesse at Liberty University graduation"

"Love that smile"

"A hero is laid to rest by his friends"

Chapter nine

Hermeneutics

HERMENEUTICS IS A BIG WORD for a simple, extremely important idea – how to study and properly interpret the Scriptures. In the dictionary it is called the science of doing that, and it's helpful to see it as an objective science, rather than as a subjective, personal approach. If we are to find the truth in God's Word, we must assume that it is there to be found, if we follow the proper, scientific guidelines that will open divine truth to the fallen human mind, which is why we need to consider hermeneutics.

The most basic concept of hermeneutics is that the Bible has only one interpretation. This is a difficult, but crucial, concept to grasp. There may be more than one application, as the Bible applies to varied situations, but there is only one basic interpretation. For example, shepherds/leaders may hear different things from John 10 than sheep/followers may hear, but the principal thought is the same for both – Jesus takes good care of His own.

This concept is critical to finding the truth in God's Word. How many times have you heard people say, in

Bible discussions, "Well, that's just your interpretation"? This is a cop out, often used as a way to end discussion, to the detriment of further learning. Agreeing to disagree is fine in relation to your favorite football team, but it is not helpful in Bible study, where we must find the truth in order to live and die properly.

As usual, Jesus deals with this in the best possible way. When He addressed issues potentially subject to various interpretations, He didn't say, "This is the right interpretation." The Bible says He opened their understanding. This is the key. We are not trying to interpret the Bible, which leads to error and division. We are trying to understand the Bible, which leads us to "the Way, the Truth and the Life." This concept is the basis for finding out what the Bible really says, which is the point of the exercise.

The first rule of hermeneutics is to begin with prayer. God's Word, shared from His heart and mind, is best understood through the help of the Holy Spirit, the One He has sent to "teach us all things." The Holy Spirit is actually excited to show us the things of God and feels grief when we leave Him on the sidelines in our study. I always begin any Bible reading or study with a simple, heartfelt prayer, "Father, teach me what you want as we come to Your Word together." It is a great blessing, during a difficult passage, to have thoughts come into my mind that obviously came from Him to help me gain a new insight, a precious part of our relationship. When we see Bible study as cherished time to get to know the One who loves us so, it becomes a joy, rather than a chore and will be that much more productive, as well.

The second rule of hermeneutics is to let the Bible say what it says. This sounds overly simplistic and obvious at first glance, but this is the rule most often overlooked, the lack of which leads to disastrous results, sandy foundations for life and dangerous heresies which actually lead people away from God, rather than pointing the way home. Too many times I have heard people say, upon reading a particular passage, "Well, I don't believe that" or "No, that's not right." This is a particularly dangerous approach, as though we, in our completely inadequate judgments, are able to tell God what is right or wrong.

To receive the full benefit of the Bible, we must let it say what it says. We must seek and, yes, even pray, to understand what God is trying to get across to us. He knows what's going on and how things work; so we should be listening to Him, rather than telling Him anything. We should always change our thinking to fit what we find in God's Word, rather than changing God's Word to fit our thinking.

If we find something hard to believe, we must accept that it is there for a purpose. To simply explain it away, because we disagree, will cause us to lose a vital part of the puzzle which God is trying to help us put together. To examine it and set it aside for future reference allows us to put it in its proper place when we progress far enough to see where it goes. Those have been some of my most treasured moments, moments of intimacy with God, when I see and understand some indispensable truth which I was going to discard because I didn't like it at first.

A corollary to this rule is to take the Bible literally unless the context indicates otherwise, unless it's evident that we're dealing with a metaphor or some other literary device, which will be obvious. Otherwise we run into the same problem of trying to decide for ourselves, which leaves us on shaky ground at best and subject to personal opinion, which will vary between people and leave us unable to find the truth. Following the guidelines given above allows us to hear what God is trying to say, and keeps us from explaining away important points we need.

Another rule is to let the Bible set the agenda and point the way as to what is important for consideration. The Bible can be used to prove any point if we set the agenda. When we come to the Bible to prove our ideas, we run the serious risk of missing the point completely, because we only see those things which say what we want to say. If we allow the Bible itself to set the agenda, we set ourselves up to discover what God thinks is important, and, in doing that, we discover the path of life.

And always remember that the best commentary on the Bible is the Bible itself. When we see an idea presented by Moses, expanded by David, demonstrated by Daniel, expounded upon by Jesus and explained by Paul, we can be pretty sure of its meaning. God has a tendency to do that with all important thoughts in the Bible. Jesus admonished people to "search the Scriptures" in order to prevent mistakes, and we should do the same, always applying the rules given previously.

The final rule is to allow ideas time to develop. Time-sensitive concepts, such as how to be saved, are simple and plainly stated for all to see and use. Deeper concepts require more time for development, often because they are based on "prerequisite" ideas, in the same way as addition and subtraction need to be mastered and expanded before even beginning to understand calculus.

If we will understand that the Bible contains kindergarten through doctoral studies all in one book, we won't get discouraged if we are only in third grade. We will find that, as we faithfully study, using the above rules, we can understand all that we need to know when we need to know it for each stage of our lives. As we cover more and more of the prerequisites, we will find the deeper concepts more readily available to our understanding, as well. Patience with this process will prevent us from getting in over our heads and keep us out of doctrinal dilemmas, as well as increasing our joy of study.

Cautionary rules of hermeneutics

There are also some cautionary rules of hermeneutics, rules of warning and restraint. These are rules which will keep us out of trouble and enable us to receive the full benefit of God's Word. Without these rules, we run the risk of distorting the message of God's word or of missing the message completely. Therefore, these rules are as important as the ones of positive approach.

The first cautionary rule is to be careful of your interpretation of a passage which you immediately like or which appears to agree with what you think. Our thought processes tend to be faulty, ego-centric and worldly. Thus, if we agree with or like a passage, it may be because it feeds our ego in some way, rather than because we have the proper understanding of it. Our first interpretation may be right, but we should always be cautious in this situation and reserve final judgment until we can find further support for our thinking, corroborating evidence elsewhere in the Bible.

Which brings us to our second cautionary rule, actually a corollary of the first. Never base an important thought or doctrine on just one reference in the Bible. If the thought is important, the Lord will cover it in other places, which will also fill out the complete concept involved. If you find what appears to be an important thought in just one place, make note of it for further reference, but don't place too much confidence in that thought until you find it developed more fully elsewhere. The Lord's principle of "in the mouth of two or three witnesses" applies in this situation as in others, for safety's sake, as there is no place you need safety as much as in your understanding of the Bible.

A third cautionary rule is to always question your "discovery" of a "new" thought, idea or concept in the

Bible, one which no one has ever thought of before. God's wonderful truths are for everyone, and He wants them understood far and wide. Sorry to say, He has not hidden some important nugget of truth away for centuries, simply so you can discover it and get famous as its discoverer. It may be new to you and exciting as such, but if other people have not already heard of it, it is probably not that important, and it may be wrong. Be careful about basing your thoughts or your life upon such a concept.

Another cautionary rule is to beware of a thought or concept which you have to pay for or involves the exchange of money somehow. God's wonderful truths are not only for everyone, they are *free* for everyone. Any time you are tempted to buy or sell an idea, be careful. There's something fishy about that, no matter how good it smells initially. When human motives get involved with God's truth, things come out funny, and it's your life and eternity on the line. So be careful. We're trying to find the truth, not a fortune.

Another cautionary rule is to beware of a teacher or of your own thoughts which will not tolerate questions. The truth can stand questions and will come out clearer and stronger for them. Jesus answered all questions, especially the tough, antagonistic ones. The book of Psalms demonstrates again and again that God is willing to answer our questions. Therefore, when you fear questions about your thinking about the Bible or find a teacher who doesn't tolerate questions, beware. Get back into the open freedom of good questions and find the light of truth which brings you into understanding of God's Word.

There are several places in the Bible which say that study of Scriptures is designed to lead us into joy and into the path of life. When we approach it that way we will truly be blessed. And when we follow these simple rules of hermeneutics, we will be able to understand the wonderful things God has for us. May God bless you as you study properly and find His heart, His thoughts and His life through His Word.

Chapter ten

Counseling

SADLY, IN MY EXPERIENCE, PEOPLE want counseling, but they don't want help. They will come for counseling to satisfy a spouse or to ease their conscience, but not to actually get help changing anything. So, over the years I've become more and more discouraged with the concept of counseling, even though I enjoy it and have been told I'm pretty good at it.

The seeds of my discouragement began when I worked at a Christian college and one of our outstanding senior students asked if she could stop by my office for a talk. She was one of those most likely to succeed people who had everything going for her, but she had begun to feel like something was wrong and wondered if I could help her figure out what it was. We had worked together for a couple of years, and she respected my opinion; so it was logical that she would come to see me, and I was delighted that she had and was sure that we could find a solution together.

My style is to listen and draw out what they are dealing with, knowing that the answer is probably already in their thoughts and experience, if I can just help them find it. It turned out that she was a business student who had done well in school and had a successful career ahead of her, but she was now feeling restless and unsettled, and was there anything I might suggest to help her? When she finished, she turned toward me expectantly.

As she had talked, it had become increasingly obvious to me what her problem was. I told her I thought the restlessness had come from the fact that she was settling for less than what God had for her, that He was calling her away from temporal things and into a deeper relationship with Himself. I suggested that she explore that idea further, and the rest would become clearer in the light of that perspective.

That wasn't what she wanted to hear. She wanted to be affirmed, rather than challenged. Although she came to me because she knew she would get an honest answer, she didn't want me to be that honest. She went away quietly and avoided me as much as she could until she graduated.

This was a great disappointment. A student had come with a situation in which there was wonderful potential for her future. Not only had I not been able to help, but I had lost a friend. It took me a while to recover.

I saw her a couple of years later when she returned to the college for an event, and her career was obviously going well. She looked the perfect picture of a successful business woman. She also looked unfulfilled and not completely at ease with herself. She was also still avoiding me. My sadness returned, thinking of what she could have been if she had heeded the Lord's upward call.

As a result of that experience, I am slower to do counseling, and I preface every session the same way. I tell them we can solve any problem together, with the Lord's help, if they are willing. Sometimes I am feeling ornery enough to tell them that the process won't work if they have ulterior motives. Sometimes, if I can already sense those other motives, I'll tell them they need to find someone else to help them. In the meantime, I love to help those who really do want to work with me and the Lord to find solutions and growth.

Basic ideas for counseling

With all this in mind, let's look at some basic ideas for counseling. First of all, and I can't emphasize this enough, the cardinal rule that must be understood is that you should be extremely slow to give personal advice, fearful that they might do what you say and get into trouble. Do you want that on your conscience?

If the Bible addresses their situation specifically, feel free to share that with them, such as, "No, I don't think it would be a good idea to rob that bank." However, to just share your opinion with someone makes you responsible for the resulting actions, and we have enough trouble trying to run our own lives, without having to be responsible for someone else's. Being careful along these lines will keep you out of a lot of trouble.

Another thing which I have experienced over the years is that people invariably know the answer to their own question. They just don't have the self-confidence or conviction to act on it. So you must listen long enough and draw them out sufficiently so that they can see that themselves. So many times they will find that they already knew the answer. They simply needed to verbalize it and have someone affirm them in doing it. To help them discover that for themselves is my idea of a successful counseling session. That also helps them take responsibility for their own decisions and actions and means that I don't have to bear that responsibility.

When there is a specific problem they want help with, people often seem to think I should help them find the root of the problem, hoping that fixing that will automatically fix the current problem. I tend to approach things differently, however, as it seems to me that reliving something from their past can be counterproductive, as it takes them back into something which was hard the first time through and shouldn't be re-introduced into their thinking. There are times when healing is needed for some trauma, and I usually recommend that they find someone who is skilled in that approach, but, in general, we take a different direction.

I favor the approach of starting from where they are and learning new thought patterns and behaviors. It seems to me that this is the Lord's approach. He can take us from wherever we are, forgive and cleanse the past, and get us started on a new and more productive path into the future. Beginning with Romans 12:1-2 and moving through Colossians 3 and the second half of Ephesians 4, I seek to help them connect with the Lord on a daily, personal level and move into newness of life with His help. If needed, we focus on specific areas, but always within that general context, which gives them a proper foundation for solving specific problems in a lasting way.

I have found that this approach is a great morale booster, as they are not beginning by focusing on their dysfunctions, which often makes them feel defective, as if they are starting already in a hole. Instead, we begin with the positive viewpoint that they can begin to make progress immediately. This concept seems to be more empowering and hopeful, as it allows them to look forward, rather than backward. People seem to have more energy to move ahead than they have to dig up a past which may have been hurtful. Beginning with the idea that they simply need to learn something new has been much more motivating than starting with the idea that they have major problems they must overcome. So this approach has great practical benefits, as well as good outcomes.

Pastoral counseling

Pastoral counseling raises problems when the counselor has ulterior motives regarding his church. To be successful, the counseling must focus on what is best for the counselee, rather than on what might or might not contribute to church growth. Guilt trips in relation to that must be avoided at all costs. Successfully and unselfishly ministering to people will always contribute to church growth in the long run. You don't have to try and help it along by devious means, simply because you have the opportunity.

Marriage counseling

Marriage counseling involves two parts – pre-marriage counseling to prepare couples for marriage and "crisis" counseling, when couples are having problems. In pre-marriage counseling, I always employ a list of "homework" questions, a series of questions designed to help the couple work through some basic concepts together. They each write out their answers separately. Then they discuss them together before I meet with them to go over the questions again, contributing some of my thoughts and experience. Designed to help them learn about and from each other and learn communication skills, this method has been enjoyable to the couples (as opposed to receiving lectures, particularly) and has had positive results.

In a side note, after using this method for some twenty years, I have tried to determine if there has been any indicator within this style of pre-marriage counseling that might predict the success or failure of the marriage. I have noticed one which I would say is consistent enough to act upon it, although I have not been brave enough yet to do so. In 100 percent of the cases, if one of the couple was not serious about doing the homework, the marriage ended in divorce. Conversely, I have worked with couples who I had concerns about, for one reason or another, and I have seen them really get into the homework, do well and even teach me some things, and they have done well in their marriages. However, I have not yet been brave enough to warn anyone whose partner is not taking the homework seriously. I like to think perhaps I might do that sometime, and I hope that you might be able to, if you encounter such a situation.

As to the crisis side of marriage counseling, there is just one simple concept, as follows. If they will put as much time, effort and money into working things out as they would put into getting a divorce, they can rebuild their marriage into a greater blessing than they have ever known. If they are serious about getting help and will apply themselves diligently to this approach, they will find it to be encouraging, hopeful and fun, and they will be blessed to watch it work. If they are not serious, nothing will work, as one or both of them will simply be looking for a way out and will short circuit the whole process.

In conclusion, counsel cautiously, prayerfully, and in complete dependence upon the Lord, and He can use you to help others find their way home to Him.

Chapter eleven

Logic

GOD HAS GIVEN US TRUTH as a solid foundation for life, and logic as a way of using truth to process thoughts, ideas and questions to come out with proper conclusions. The universe is held together by logic, because it is held together by Jesus, Who is the Truth. As a result, any math problem, from simple addition to the most complicated calculus, will give you the same answer every time. The moon will be right where it is supposed to be when the astronauts arrive looking for it. And God's consistent and logical actions and reactions make a firm foundation for faith. It is only when we move away from logic that things don't make sense, and our lives begin to fall apart.

A commitment to the truth is the key to logic. Ideas must be conformed to the truth to begin to make sense of them. It's when we try to bend the truth to fit our ideas that we get into trouble, as that is the root of irrational. At that point we begin to move out of touch with reality and should not be surprised when things no longer fit, and the results become erratic and unpredictable.

However, when we base our thinking on the truth as revealed in God's Word and in the person of Christ, our thoughts begin to move in conjunction with reality, which means they will fit with the world around us, and we can predict the results. That is a simple description of logic, which is essential to making sense of life and our place in it. It even helps us deal with the unreality and irrationality of the thoughts and actions of those around us, as we will be anchored in reality and will be able to withstand the storms of weirdness kicked up by that irrationality.

In a sense, logic is simply common sense, although one friend commented that there is nothing as uncommon as common sense. Logic is the natural progression of thoughts, one thought rationally leading to the next, uninterrupted by an outside agenda. If you are not trying to prove something outside of the truth, thought process will flow naturally to the proper conclusion. If you begin with a conclusion and try to build a thought process to prove it, logic often goes out the window, and the aimless wandering which results has a tendency to send you into left field somewhere, with no hope of finding your way home. Logic is a gift of God, as natural as breathing and just as essential to life. It's when we pervert it and try to make it do our bidding that we lose its life-directing power.

Even Jesus was bound by logic and expected His hearers to operate within its bounds as they considered what He was telling them. In fact, He was one of the few great teachers in history to tell His listeners *not* to believe Him if what He said didn't make sense (John 10:37-38).

Of course, the opposite was true, as well – if what He said did make sense, which it always did to the objective listener, then, naturally, they should believe Him.

Use of reason

So, how do you apply logic and make it work for you to help you arrive at the proper conclusions? In the simplest terms – you begin with the truth, and stay there throughout your thought process. Truth always begets truth, and thus the process will flow to its natural conclusion. Discard any outside agendas or opinions which are not truth-based, after proper examination in light of the truth. Follow common sense to its obvious conclusion, and wind up in the right place naturally.

Let's look at Jesus as an example, since He bound Himself to logic. He came into the world claiming to be God in the flesh. This doesn't make sense, except for these six things: 1) His coming was a fulfillment of thousands of years of prophecy; 2) Angels announced His birth publicly (to Mary and Joseph and the shepherds); 3) Wise men came from the east seeking the newborn king, whose sign they had seen in the heavens, signs confirmed by scholars in Jerusalem who knew the very town of His birth; 4) He acted like God in relation to the natural world (He healed the sick, controlled the wind, raised the dead, etc.; 5) He told people personal things about themselves and others which only God would know, with deep wisdom only God would have;

6) He announced that He would die, then rise again the third day, and He did just as He said.

In light of all this evidence, what Jesus said does make sense. Only God could do the things that He did over and over again, no flukes. So logic, unhindered by any outside agenda, leads us to the conclusion that He actually was who He said He was, God in the flesh.

Applied to any other problem or thought process, logic will lead you from truth to truth until the conclusion is apparent, just as it does in solving more complicated math problems. This will happen naturally if you do not allow agendas or opinions, either yours or those of others, to move you away from the truth along the way. It's actually a very simple and liberating thing to find the truth so easily in a world distorted by multiple opinions and agendas, although sometimes it takes a while to sort through all those conflicting ideas thrust upon you.

System of thought

To take advantage of the blessings of logic in every day life, you must commit yourself to the proper system of thought. You must commit yourself to the truth, no matter where it may lead you. You must commit yourself to the rejection of falsehoods, no matter how attractive they may appear at the time. You must commit yourself to following the natural progression of truth, as that is the only sure path to a solid, life-affirming conclusion.

Logic only works in a reality-based system of thought. It's often pleasant to develop your own reality, live in "your own little world". However, when this is the case, you should not be surprised when certain parts of that world don't make sense. And you will also find that logic won't do you any good, because it will forever be bumping up against the brick wall of unreality, and there will be no way around.

So commit yourself to a reality-based system of thought. You will find that logic works well within that system. Logic comes naturally within that system, as progression of thought from one to the next flows smoothly when guided by truth. And when you hit a bump of confusion along the way, clear away the unreality detours, and the way will become clear again.

Logic is simple enough for any properly motivated person to use. In fact, children often astound adults with their ease in the use of logic. However, logic may not always be easy, as so many agendas make demands upon us and confuse the truth. But if we will commit ourselves to a truth-based system of thought, logic will come more and more easily with practice, and we will be able to enjoy its blessings in our life and decisions.

Breaking out of Jonah thinking

There are times when we get trapped in Jonah thinking and need God's help to break out of it. Jonah thinking, as illustrated by the book of Jonah, is small thinking, restricted by our personal feelings and experiences, unable to see a bigger picture. Jonah thinking results in poor choices which are too often counterproductive and short range in their vision.

Jonah didn't like Nineveh, and with good reason. However, allowing his feelings and experiences to guide his choices, rather than seeking God's perspective, caused him to move away from God's best, be satisfied with less, and wind up in the dark with seaweed wrapped around his head. This is a rather drastic picture of what we each will face, in one way or another, when we do the same thing in our lives, ignoring God's revealed plan.

Because of His amazing grace, God may not allow us to stay stuck in Jonah thinking, for which I am very thankful. As He did with Jonah, He brings things into our lives designed to break us out of Jonah thinking, help us see things from His perspective and bring us into a place of blessing again. Jonah's limited perspective was washed away (literally), and he moved (however reluctantly) into God's far-reaching plan to rescue 120,000 people who needed redemption, although he was rather slow to comprehend what had happened.

So when we allow ourselves to be restricted by our experiences and feelings, we should not be surprised if God does something to break us out. He constantly desires to have us leave our small, albeit comfortable, world behind and move out into His wide and wonderful world. It ought to be our desire, as well, to leave our little plans behind and go with Him into His awesome, life-changing plans. I hope this raises your awareness, as I would hate for you to miss out.

Chapter twelve

Ethics

ETHICS ARE THE PRINCIPLES, MORALS and beliefs that, in the final analysis, determine who we are. Without ethics we are animals or machines without a command system. Ethics are your basic framework for life, actions and decision making, the root cause for all that you think or do. Ethics are your internal compass; your guiding force which will take you through any circumstances or situation and bring you out in the right place.

Ethics are not rules, regulations or laws, although they may be made into rules or laws. Ethics are about the internal guidance system of the heart and mind, unaffected and unenforced by external law. Ethics are about who you are when you are alone.

When I think of that, I always think of a hired hand my father had on his farm. That man was a hard worker, conscientious and reliable. Because of that, he was often sent out to do a job on the farm by himself, unsupervised. One day my father went out to check on his progress and found him working harder than he would when they were working together. When questioned about that, he gave the answer that he didn't want them to think that he only worked hard when they were around. In other words, his ethics came from his principles, not from their supervision.

I also think about Jesse when he was going into the Marine Corps. I told him that he did not have to obey any command that contradicted his conscience. In fact, I think the Marines have it written into their code of conduct that you must refuse an unlawful command. I told Jesse that if more soldiers had done that down through the centuries, it would have neutralized the power of evil dictators, as they would have had no one to carry out their unlawful, unethical commands against society.

I knew that Jesse was so conscientious that he would probably do even more than he was asked to do by any lawful command. But I also wanted him to know that it was okay to follow his conscience, knowing that any punishment for that would not, could not be worse than living with a failure to stand for what was right. That, in a nutshell, are what ethics are all about.

There is a tendency to focus on fringe issues of ethics, rather than on the foundation or the root of ethics; to debate "greater good vs. the lesser of two evils", etc., rather than to explore the source. However, since ethics are primarily concerned with and flow out of the internal guidance system, this is where the focus needs to be. Take care of that, and the fringe issues will take care of themselves.

Paul said it best. "I beseech you, therefore, brethren, by the mercies of God, that you present your bodies a living sacrifice, holy, acceptable unto God, which is your reasonable service. And don't be conformed to this world: but be transformed by the renewing of your mind, that you may prove what is that good, and acceptable, and perfect will of God" (Romans 12:1-2). In other words, make sure your internal compass is properly aligned, and you'll know the right thing in any situation. Trying to foresee and discuss every possible situation leads to confusion and misses the main point, anyway.

If you commit yourself to do what's right, i.e., to do things the Lord's way, ethical decision making is much easier. If you are in the habit of doing the right thing, it will be easier to do the right thing. If you are always looking for the right thing to do, it will become second nature to determine the right thing to do. And I just realized that this is a description of how Jesse approached life.

If you are simply living by rules, you'll have a tendency to bend the rules to fit the situation. And if you are always looking for loopholes, you will probably find them, and your ethical decision making process becomes much more difficult. If you have to make decisions situation by situation (I believe that's called "situational ethics"), you will have no compass and will simply do whatever feels good at the moment and find yourself way off track without being able to understand why it happened. The '60's and the resulting chaos are an excellent large scale example of the fallacy of that approach.

The critical thing about ethics is to have them in place *before* you need them. If you wait until you're in the middle of a serious situation before you try to decide what to do, it's already too late and could bring disastrous consequences. If you develop your ethics pre-emptively and commit to the decisions you have made, you will have a solid starting point for any choice you have to make and will more likely make a good choice.

The Bible tells us that a double minded person is unstable. I take this to mean that if you have to think twice ("Do I do the right thing? Or do I do the convenient thing?") before making a decision, you're in trouble to start with. If your heart is settled on doing the right thing whatever decisions you may face, this eliminates the pressure and confusion of the moment and allows you to objectively process the input and come up with a sensible solution which is guided by what you actually want to do, rather than by the stress of the situation. Jesse was particularly adept at this, always guided by the sure foundational precepts of a meticulously formed set of ethics.

This brings us to the source of that internal guidance system, the resource we need to form our ethics properly in an unethical world. Ideally, this internal guidance system would align with reality in a way which would allow us to make our way through the maze of unreality which often surrounds us and come out with good choices which would shape our lives in good ways. To be successful with integrity would be a good measure of the value of our ethics.

The best way to integrate with reality is to get to know Jesus, the source of reality; the One Who said simply, "I am the Way, the Truth, and the Life". Paul said Jesus was "the fullness of the Godhead bodily". We have the opportunity to get to know Him personally, even to "have the mind of Christ". Now, there's an internal guidance system which will see us through anything and bring us out in the right place. As we get to know Him, allowing His heart and thoughts to fill and transform our thinking, His ethics become our ethics, and "the Light of the world" illuminates the dark paths we must travel. Choices become obvious. Decisions become simple. Inner strength and integrity become the norm. Situations bend to our ethics, rather than the other way around.

Again, I think of Jesse. In a Marine environment geared to molding people to their standards, Jesse embraced the standard of excellence and then embodied a higher standard in his personal life. He was a good Marine, company high shooter in boot camp, always studying his Marine guidebooks, always pushing himself to do better, to the extent that he made sergeant in just over three years, a tough thing for a reservist. And yet, when buddies tried to push him into "other Marine activities", even threatening to gang up on him to make him join in on their drinking and carousing, he politely, but forcefully, stood for what he thought was right and exemplified what a good Marine could be without that. Who he was inside came through, and they respected him for that. That, in a nutshell, is what ethics are all about.

So, get to know Jesus. Let His heart and mind transform yours. As you study His Word, ask Him to implant

His reality-based ethics in your heart. Determine from the outset to do the right thing in every situation. With that internal guidance system to direct you, the way will become clear in any situation, and the fringe issues will resolve themselves.

Chapter thirteen

Discipleship

JESUS, THE GREAT DISCIPLER, SAID, "All authority is given unto Me in heaven and on earth. Go therefore and make disciples of all nations..." If Jesus said this as part of the great commission, then the concept of discipleship must be rather important and bears considering as we ponder His ministry and our ministry in His name. He is also the most important example of the method of discipleship necessary for transforming lives and the world. This chapter is meant to be a general discussion of His example, rather than a detailed outline of any particular method. I trust this may be helpful in developing your own approach to discipleship.

There are many fine programs of discipleship which have been helpful in the personal growth of Christians worldwide. I am thankful for each of these programs and for their ministry in helping to fulfill the great commission. However, in this setting, I will be examining solely the method Jesus used, as a foundation for our thinking about discipleship, as this is the only one I have tried and thus the only one with which I am familiar. I have found that it results in good disciples, able to stand on their own and to help others find a vital relationship with the Savior, as well.

It begins with a choice, a commitment. Jesus asked the original disciples to follow Him, knowing that if it was not their decision to do so, He could not and would not force them to be his disciples. He even asked them to renew their commitment later, when so many others decided they didn't want to follow any more, "Will you also go away?" When they responded, "To whom shall we go? You have the words of eternal life", their training continued.

In fact, as we read through the Gospels, we see Jesus turning away many potential disciples in whom was lacking the complete commitment which was required. This, then, is the first concept of discipleship. We would do better to make it harder than easier to sign on to follow Christ; so that any potential disciples go into it with their eyes wide open and will not be surprised when the going gets tough later on. Jesus had a tendency to do this right up front, being explicit about the difficulties involved, obviously willing to have fewer, more committed disciples, rather than striving for larger numbers of fair weather friends.

With these committed disciples, Jesus' first step was to teach by example. He took them everywhere with Him, letting them hear Him, watch Him, ask Him questions. So book learning is important, but don't forget the labs. He let them see how all the things He was teaching actually worked in real life. We must exemplify what it means to follow Jesus if we want others to take up the path, as well.

The next step was experience of their own, with the authority and responsibility that went with it. He sent the twelve out on their own. He gave them detailed instructions and then sent them out to teach and heal and minister in His name, to experience how it worked for themselves. Later, He sent out seventy more the same way, to learn by doing, and they returned full of joy and empowered to take on the world. As a result of this stage of the training, we find, not just twelve, but 120 disciples meeting in the upper room after the resurrection, waiting for Pentecost.

This method builds morale, as well as motivation. One of the student advisors under me at the Christian college where I worked came to me for a suggestion about how to make this work in the dorm where he served. I suggested that they start a nursing home ministry, which is always any easy first step of ministry. I went with them the first couple of times to show them how things worked and then turned them loose to carry on themselves. They had an experience like that of the seventy in the Gospels. They returned with joy for what they had seen God do through them and empowered to move into the next steps of following Jesus in their lives.

The next part of Jesus' discipleship program involved simply taking the time needed for all these things to amalgamate in the minds and hearts of the disciples. It was a three year course, not a three week course, with lots of times for questions, experiences and teachable moments. It actually did not seem to be very structured, simply interwoven through daily life in a way which made sense each step of the way and built toward a cohesive whole. Our modern culture militates against such an approach, but understanding this basic concept will help us apply it in our ministries is a relevant way. Let us take the time necessary to understand and apply what Jesus demonstrated.

Then Jesus summed it all up for the disciples in the week or two of teaching before His death. He gave them the blueprint for the church. He gave them a physical connection to Himself in the institution of the Lord's Supper which would serve as a constant reminder of His presence and ministry for the next two thousand years. He prayed for them in their presence. He had several sessions of personal review for them after His resurrection, and He gave them the gift of the Spirit to seal the deal and empower them for the task He had given them to do. And, in giving them the full responsibility, He expressed His confidence in their ability to fulfill it, an encouraging affirmation which also empowered them.

So we see that Jesus' method of discipleship, though not highly structured, was comprehensive and personal, and we would do well to learn from His example. We can offer the same thing to those who are willing to take an active part in the process. We can exemplify what it means to follow Christ. We have full access to His Word and the Spirit to teach and empower. There are plenty of opportunities for hands-on learning and instructive experiences. If we take the necessary time to work with interested people and take advantage of teachable moments, we can help people understand how things work for themselves. We can pass on what has been passed on to us and thus make disciples of those who desire to know and follow Jesus.

References: - Christ's call: Matthew 4:18-22 - the re-commitment: John 6:67-71 - challenging commitment: Luke 9:57-62 - sharing experiences: Mark 5:35-43, Luke 9:12-36 -experience of their own: Matthew 10, Luke 10 - summary: John 13-16 - blue print for the church: John 15 - established reminder: Luke 22 - prayed for them: John 17 - post-resurrection review: Luke 24, John 21 - Spirit to empower: John 16, Acts 1:8, Acts 2, etc. – full responsibility: Matthew 28:18-20, Mark 16:15, Acts 1:8, etc.

Chapter fourteen

Revival

WHENEVER SOMEONE TELLS ME THEY are praying for revival for the church, I cannot resist giving them my standard response. I always say I am praying for tribulation and persecution for the church. And then I explain. Throughout history the church has been strongest, grown the most, experienced revival most often during times of tribulation and persecution; so isn't that what we should be praying for? Most people have no response to that, except to shrug and say, "I suppose so."

The reason I give that response and get that response is because of the modern application of the concept of revival. It has come to mean kind of a magical intervention by God to enliven the church and to renew the country so we can all live happily ever after. This is what most people are looking for, so they don't look further into the Biblical concepts. They simply keep praying and hoping (and wondering why revival never seems to come).

This morning I was reading Psalms 79-81. In 79 and 80, the psalmist is moaning and groaning and pleading with God to rescue His people, punish their enemies, and bring revival. In 81, he comes back to reality, looks at Israel's history of disregard for the Lord, and realizes that they didn't really want God to have His way with them, a way which would have brought tremendous blessing. This is the problem in a nutshell. Prayer cannot replace obedience as the key to revival.

The current verse of choice in relation to revival is 2 Chronicles 7:14. You know the one, "If My people... pray...I will...heal their land." Again, prayer is substituted for obedience, and they wonder why revival doesn't come. They ignore the most critical parts of that verse, the reason that verse was even given to us – the "... humble themselves...seek my face, and turn from their wicked ways..." parts. They ignore the obedience parts and wonder why God seems to ignore their prayers.

The very word, revival, indicates that something is wrong, that life needs to be breathed back into the dead. In the Bible, it is used in reference to a sinful and wandering people in need of repentance and resuscitation. To be praying for revival for your church is an indictment of your church. You are a part of that church, and thus it is an indictment of yourself.

I have always thought that we should focus on vival, rather than re-vival. We should concentrate on living faithful, obedient lives that keep us in the center of God's best for us; so we won't have to be revived. This is Jesus living. He never had a revival, because He didn't need one. We shouldn't need one either, because we should be enjoying daily the abundant life He said He came to give. With all that in mind, I hope we wake up and never have another revival.

Chapter fifteen

Theology

THEOLOGY, AS A CONCEPT, HAS come to include more
than simply the study of God, which the word implies.
It has been broadened to incorporate both the study
of God and how we relate to Him, and we will examine
both of these thoughts briefly in this chapter. Much
has been written about them in exhaustive formats in
massive tomes, and I will not attempt to replicate the
fine work of others. In the spirit of what Jesse asked me
to do, I will hopefully point you in the right direction
for further personal study, study designed to help you
know God in a way which will enrich your life, as Jesse
desired for himself and intended for others.

Reflections of God

Jesus said no one has seen God at any time. As we
watch encounters with God throughout the Bible, we
begin to understand why. God is too overwhelming for
our human senses to process properly. Thus, we see
people knocked flat, blinded, blown over unconscious,

etc. when coming face to face with the presence of God. Therefore, in order to give us some means of "seeing" Him, He has given us the opportunity to see reflections of Him, in ways which our feeble hearing and seeing can handle, process and understand. This method is one which anyone who has ever looked into a mirror or a calm mountain lake can comprehend and appreciate.

Paul explains this concept fairly comprehensively in the first chapter of Romans. He says that that which may be known about God is discernible in us; because God has showed it to us. He says that the invisible things of God can be seen and understood from the world around us, even His eternal power and Godhead. In this way, we "see" God and can begin to understand Him and His way of being and doing as it relates to us.

We see His beauty, goodness and grace reflected in a warm spring morning which is bursting with life. We see His majesty reflected in a mountain sunrise or a sunset over crashing breakers driving into seaside cliffs. We see His power reflected in a thunderstorm or earthquake or in a wind which can demolish the best we can build or drive a shaft of straw through a sheet of plywood. We see His love reflected in a mother's eyes as her basic mothering instincts embrace her helpless little ones. We see His careful guidance reflected in the passing flocks of geese traveling unerringly to their winter nesting grounds. And the list is endless, reflections of God in the world around us, despite the worst we sinners have done to push them away. If we will gaze with open hearts at the world around us, we will see endless, enlightening reflections of God which will allow us to begin to understand who He is and what He can and wants to do in the world and in our lives.

Glimpses of God

The whole theme of the Bible is that God delights to be known. He knows you and wants you to know Him. In the Garden of Eden, we find God actively involved in each day, from the creative and teaching processes to the evening visits with His creation. Through this He demonstrates that He expects to be a part of everyday life. We were created to live best as we live with Him, depending upon His input, His wisdom, His strength. All of this assumes that we would just naturally get to know God as an ordinary part of life.

That process was disrupted when Adam and Eve decided to go their own way. Now we have to depend on God's gracious revelations of Himself, in order to get reacquainted. Thankfully, God has chosen to reveal Himself to us is through His Word given to special people chosen according to specific, objective guidelines. The Bible has many places where it simply tells us what God is like, such as "God is love". However, it fills out our understanding of God by giving us glimpses of Him as He acts and interacts in our world.

This is the way we get to know characters in any book we read. We are usually given a basic description of the person; but then we get to know them, their personalities, their thought processes, their ways of being, as we see them act and interact throughout the story. We are offered that same opportunity in God's Word, glimpses of Him in settings and situations we can understand; so we can get to know Him.

We get a glimpse of His justice, love and forgiveness as we watch Him deal with Adam and Eve after their blatant disobedience, which helps us understand His approachableness, even though we have wandered away. We get a glimpse of His righteous anger with sin which resulted in the worldwide judgment in the flood, which helps us feel secure in the knowledge that good will triumph over evil. We get a glimpse of His willingness to be involved in our lives as we watch Him extend the offer of personal friendship to Abraham. We get a glimpse of His redemptive power as we watch Him bring Israel out of bandage and into the Promised Land and understand that He could even redeem us. We get a glimpse of His commitment to truth and righteousness as we watch Him write the Ten Commandments on tablets of stone, which helps us understand the importance of doing things the right way. We get a glimpse of His personal care in bringing Daniel out of the lion's den and Peter out of prison, which helps us understand that He is ready to help us.

The list of examples goes on and on, glimpses of God in settings and situations we can relate to; so we can "see" and understand God in new and personal ways. In these glimpses of God we begin to understand Him and how He wants to be involved in our lives. We begin to get a comprehensive picture of God which enables us to understand how to trust Him and how to relate to Him, a blessed thought and privilege which we ought to take advantage of and for which we will be eternally grateful. However, these reflections and glimpses are only the beginning of God's gracious revelation of Himself to us in order for us to be able to share His life.

The Ultimate Reflection

The final expression of God's willingness to be known is wrapped up in the person of Jesus, "the fullness of the Godhead bodily", the Ultimate Reflection in a world of reflections of God. As a means of revealing Himself in a way we can truly see and understand, Jesus is perfect. People could see Him, hear Him, touch Him and relate to Him in ordinary ways which allowed them to comprehend God in their terms and understand how approachable He was, and if they had a question, they could ask Him. What an amazing concept! Jesus said, "If you have seen Me, you have seen the Father."

People found what they were looking for, seeing the predictable power of God, when they saw Jesus heal the sick, calm the storm and raise the dead; but they also saw the true nature of God when they watched Jesus touch a leper, forgive a harlot, minister to an occupying centurion. They felt the love of God as they watched Jesus bless the children, raise the widow's only son and have lunch with Zaccheus, the collaborator; but they also felt the anger of God as they watched Jesus cleanse the temple and call hypocritical religious leaders vipers and whitewashed sepulchers. They saw the righteousness of God as they watched Jesus fulfill the law to the letter while offering mercy within the law in dealing with the woman caught in adultery; but they also saw the justice of God as they watched Jesus publicly point out the sinfulness of her accusers.

Repeatedly, and in a variety of settings and situations, people saw the person, purpose and power of the invisible God reflected in the fully observable life of Jesus. It was all recorded so we, too, could begin to see and understand what God is like by watching what Jesus is like. And it was shared with us in such a way that we can actually experience and learn to relate to God Himself.

The opportunity for personal experience

These three ways of getting to know God are about knowing God from a distance, knowing *about* God. However, because of His desire for an intimate relationship with His creation, God offers yet another way. He has come to us with an opportunity for us to get to know Him personally; so the question of knowing Him can be settled once and for all through personal experience, heart proof which offers assurance like no other.

People seem to think it good sport to debate with me the existence of God, somehow thinking that if they can outsmart me that would prove that He does not exist. (This has always amazed me, since it seems to me that faith should be based upon what is true, rather than upon whether or not they are cleverer than I am.) Because of this phenomenon, I have matched wits with some very clever people, some of whom have spent a lot of time and effort trying to prove the non-existence of God. They have fully developed arguments which make a lot of sense to them and satisfy them that God is not there for them to have to answer to, and they delight to stump me with their clever ideas. However, they always hit an insurmountable wall when I tell them that, although I may not be able to out debate them, I know for sure that God is there, because He has come into my life, and I have gotten to know Him personally.

God offers that same opportunity to each of us. Jesus demonstrated it throughout His ministry, and then summed it up rather dramatically in some of His last words to us, "Behold, I stand at the door and knock. If anyone hears My voice, and opens the door, I will come in and eat with him, and he with me." What an opportunity!!! Throughout the centuries, every single person, no matter how great or small, who sincerely took Him up on that offer, experienced the joy of having Jesus, God in the flesh, come into their life to share with them in intimate ways only hinted at by the eating together analogy.

In another place in this book, I have told about how God introduced Himself to me. I believe He introduces Himself to us in personal ways so that we will know that He is there and is interested in having us get to know Him, kind of an ice breaker experience. However, the next step in the relationship is prolonged personal contact which enables us to get to know Him. For me, this process began at a career weekend at a Christian college in Texas.

At this stage of my life, I knew I was lost – purpose-less and aimless with no hope of finding someone who could help me find my way. Over the course of the weekend, I heard, in many different ways from many different people, that God cared about me and was interested in getting involved in my life personally. This was a radically different concept from what I had learned in church as a child, that God loved the whole world, but kind of from a distance, definitely not in a way which involved any kind of personal relationship.

The concept that Jesus came not just to love the world, but to love me and be my Savior, was a delightful new thought. Throughout the weekend, there grew in me an increasing desire to partake of that idea some-how. Then, on the last afternoon we were there, a young man approached me with the information I needed to make that a reality.

He was making incredible statements, pointing out the references in the Bible. He said that if I would invite Jesus to come into my life, I could get to know the Savior personally and have Him be my Friend and Guide for the rest of my life. Talk about a radical approach to knowing that God was real! This was it – either the whole thing was a fairy tale or I would actually meet Jesus, God in the flesh, that very afternoon.

We now take a short break from the story to exam-ine what was at stake and how it relates to theology, the study of God. This young man was not trying to convert me to his religion. He was not trying to convince me through the clever use of debater's skills. He was offering to introduce me to God Himself.

If God was not there, the whole thing would not work, and the young man's reality would collapse. If God was there, and the young man had represented Him accurately, I would meet Him in person that afternoon and enter into a whole new level of reality. This was no longer a theoretical exercise, but a life and death, where the rubber hits the road, kind of situation, one which no sane person would offer to another unless he was absolutely sure of the outcome. This was the ultimate test of whether or not God was there and whether or not we can get to know Him.

Back to the story – from my heart I asked Jesus to come into my life… and He came into my life so sweetly and completely that I knew for sure that my life would never be the same. You may try to psychoanalyze my experience, but you will never be able to explain away what happened to me that afternoon in a Texas college dormitory, especially since it has been confirmed by the Lord's gracious presence in my life over and over again since then.

It works, because God is there and has made provisions for us to get to know him. It has been my unending joy to pass that on to others since then and watch Jesus come into their lives when they ask Him. There is no other requirement. I have watched Jesus come into the life of a man in jail for murder and saw his life transformed in that instant and on into the months ahead.

I have watched Jesus come into the life of a 103-year-old woman who had been waiting a long time to hear and understand so she could get to know Him. I saw three-year-old Jesse ask Jesus to come into his life, and Jesus did just that in such a way that Jesse never doubted it or strayed from it, although we were extremely intentional about not pushing him, always encouraging him in his own relationship with the Lord, independent of ours. And he passed that on to many others who found the Lord through his ministry, because it works!

Thus, in these four ways, God reveals Himself to us, available for the knowing. He lays it out for us in creation, in His Word and in the Person of Jesus. Then He gives us the opportunity to get to know Him personally. It remains for us to take advantage of this opportunity

Applied theology

We have a tendency to think that theology is for old men to consider, ideally in a monastery, but not for us to worry about. However, we cannot escape it. We are all theological beings, living, thinking, acting and reacting according to our personal theology, our perception of God and how we relate to Him.

All of the good things which have ever been done in the world have been done because of someone's theology. America was founded as it was because of the theology of the founding fathers, who believed

God was willing to be involved and that man was basically a collection of sinners who needed checks and balances in order to begin to enjoy freedom properly. Mother Teresa did what she did for the poor because she believed God cared for them and that she could make a difference for them. People care for us because they believe there is a caring God out there Who they should emulate.

All of the terrible things which have ever been done have been done because of someone's theology. Hitler's atrocities came out of faulty theology which caused him to believe that he, rather than God, was in control, and that God placed a lower value on the life and dignity of different classes and races. Stalin's atrocities came out of the faulty theology which caused him to believe that God did not exist, that humans were simply animals, that power was the deciding factor and that he would not have to give account to anyone for his actions. People have oppressed others for centuries because of faulty theology which caused them to believe wrong things about God and about their responsibility to Him and their fellow human beings.

Bad theology not only sets people on the wrong path, it undermines their thought processes, hindering rational thinking which would lead to recovery and a good life. This is why people with a faulty theology have a tendency to get farther and farther into trouble. Good theology not only sets people on the right path to begin with, it under girds their thought processes, leading to rational thinking which leads to good choices and a good life. This is why these people seem blessed and are often envied or persecuted by the others, who can't understand why they have "have it so easy".

Therefore, the key to good living is a good theology. This is the reason God has gone to such lengths to give us good theology. It is vital to our lives and to the life of the planet to have our theology in order. Consequently, this is one of the most critical chapters for our consideration. Good theology, a good foundation for how to relate to God once we have come to know Him, is vital.

One of the main problems with theology is that just the sound of the word is ominous and deep, as though God is far away and hides couched in big words and musty tomes of incomprehensible theories. Sometimes theologians, in order to impress people, perpetuate this concept by speaking and writing ponderously, complicating things to the point that only they can understand, which gives them their own comfort zone. God, however, approaches things completely differently. He is wise enough to make the complicated simple, because our lives and eternities depend upon our understanding of the important things of God and how they relate to us.

For me, all of theology is summed up in what Jesus called the greatest commandments, to love God with all that you are and to love the people around you. Seeking to live these two concepts will put our lives in order and will put all of our living into the proper perspective. We will experience the life and joy that God has for us and will be a blessing to those around us. Paul said that all of the law is fulfilled in these two concepts; so there it is in a nutshell, a simple description of applied theology which we can understand and use in our daily lives.

So, how do we love God with all that we are? We simply think, act and react with Him in mind in everything we do; the same way we would love anyone else. In this way, we will make right choices and do the right things, honoring Him, which He knows will give us a good life. It is so characteristic of God to ask us to do something for Him which will result in good things for us.

And just as it is easy to love someone who is good to us, it becomes easier and easier to love God as we get to know Him more through the methods described above. As we learn how much God loves us, it is easy to honor Him in all we think and do. As we learn how He has our best in mind and is ready to help us achieve it, it is easy to choose things which would please Him. As we understand more and more of His gracious purposes, it is easy to love Him in practical ways which will bless us as they bless Him. All of the laws concerning relations with God in the Bible are merely the details of this concept.

The second concept of applied theology is similar – loving others as ourselves. This fulfills all the law of God, as it will keep us from hurting others and guides us in helping others, which is God's design for interpersonal relationships. All of the laws about interpersonal relations in the Bible are merely the details of this concept.

This basically boils down to being intentional in our relations with others, thoughtfully choosing our actions and reactions, with their best interests in mind.

Ironically, this course of action also makes life better for us, so characteristic of God's design. Treating people well usually elicits good treatment from them. Reacting gently often dissipates anger and bad feelings. Graciousness often results in gracious responses. This is applied theology at its best, making a positive difference in our lives and in the world around us.

In conclusion, good theology is crucial. It is the basis for our being, for a good life, and for a blessed eternity. Understanding this, God goes out of His way to make Himself available to be known, even after we have constantly pushed Him away. And after we do get to know Him, He guides us in applied theology, that we may share the intended blessings of His creation. May God bless you as you grow in your understanding of this concept.

Chapter sixteen

Missions

Jesus said specifically, in at least two different contexts, "Go into all the world and preach the Gospel to everyone." In many other contexts and other ways, He said we should share the Gospel with the whole world. The reason for this is simple. Throughout the Bible, from beginning to end, one of the major themes is that God's good news is to be shared with the whole world. Redemption is for everyone, and they all need to hear about it; so they'll have a chance to receive it.

The call to missions

If you're looking for a call to missions, that was it! End of discussion; question settled. If God's recurring theme and Christ's specific command are not enough, then you'll never hear one. The idea that we need a personal call before we would consider being a missionary is the opposite of the Biblical concept. The Bible places a personal missionary call on the life of each and every follower of Jesus! What we really need is a personal call to stay home before we should even consider that option.

Everywhere the Gospel is preached, this concept is understood intuitively – this good news is meant to be shared. I read about a tribe in South America which received the Gospel and began to have a burden for their neighboring tribes, the natural outcome of receiving such good news. Without being told, they sent missionaries over the mountains to speak to the tribe in the next valley. They were received with joy, and that tribe responded to the gracious news of redemption, as well.

It wasn't until later, when the original missionary visited that other tribe, that he discovered that they spoke an entirely different language. Somehow, the Holy Spirit had bridged the gap; but then, that shouldn't really be a surprise. In the great commission, Jesus said He would provide the power, a thought which He repeated when He sent forth the church in Acts 1:8.

So, go! It is the Lord's command. He is ready to provide the power and will do so in response to our obedience. Can you imagine what the world would be like if every believer had to find a reason to stay home, rather than needing a reason to go to some mission field?

A personal example

In college I was pursuing a missionary career, in response to the Lord's Biblical command. I trained in Bible, anthropology, linguistics, missionary medicine, radio and missionary technology. I got involved in youth ministry, Bible studies, mission societies and jail ministry, in order to learn about mission work and to get practical experience. I got my passport and my shots and did a summer internship with a missionary in Colombia, South America. I did everything I could think of to prepare to serve the Lord overseas.

Then came our annual spring mission's conference in my last semester at college. I spent much time in prayer, assuming that if God was ready to lead me to my assignment; it would probably be during this conference. I listened carefully to the speakers. I visited the displays of the different mission groups represented there. And I received a strong, clear calling to go home. So I went home after graduation, assuming that this was the next step along the way to foreign service.

The Lord had something else in mind. He provided a job which gave me an opportunity to minister to local college students. I had the opportunity to lead to the Lord the young lady who would later become my wife. And, in following His leading, the Lord was able to lead me into my life's work as a pastor in this country. He blessed me with a family and a place of ministry which fit my temperament and gifts in a way which best fit His purposes and supported His ministry of sharing the Gospel with the world at the same time. There may be an overseas assignment in my future, but, for now, I am serving where He wants me, and He is blessing my efforts.

In the meantime, we have always supported friends whom He led into foreign service. We have supported them financially and in prayer. Every believer who is called to stay home should do that; so we each fulfill our responsibility as part of God's team to share the Gospel with the world.

Message for the world

One important thing to remember about Christ's command to go into all the world is that we are not only supposed to take a message *to* the world; we are supposed to take a message *for* the world. In other words, we are not supposed to be exporting our culture to change other cultures. The message Jesus gave us applies to every culture, because it is above culture. It is a message of the heart, rather than a message about any exterior issue. When we get confused about this concept, we dilute the power of the Gospel, hinder the work of the Spirit, and do a disservice to those for whom we deliver the message.

The message is simple, addressing basic human needs, rather than trying to reform their culture or their country. No matter the country or the culture, we are all lost, in need of redemption. Nevertheless, God still loves us and gave His Son to redeem us. Jesus died on the cross, rose again, and lives forevermore to offer salvation to whosoever, from any culture, country or background, receives Him as their own. This is the message which speaks to the world, no matter what country or culture.

And Jesus, in the great commission, told us to teach the world the things He taught us, not the things our culture teaches us. We would do well to stick with "Love God with all your heart, and love your neighbor as yourself." This addresses the deepest needs of the human heart, no matter what country or culture they live in. This is why Jesus gave us that message for the world. This is the message the world needs to hear, and this is what missionary work is all about. Anything less is merely social services or reform work.

Anybody can do reform work, but we are the only ones who can take Christ's message to the world. Only those who know Him and have experienced His redeeming work in their lives can truly share it with others. Therefore, it is up to us. Unless, we do it, it won't get done, and the world will remain in darkness. The world awaits.

The method is crucial, as well. Jesus did not come to straighten us out. He came to love us back to the Father. This should be our approach, as well. We have a natural tendency to want to straighten people out, but that's not the point. Redemption is the key. If we will go lovingly into the world to share the message of redemption, the natural results will be straightened out people and maybe even radically changed culture: but that must come from the inside out. Our responsibility is to lead people to Christ and let Him lead them to change.

Jesus commands us to go. We are the only ones who can do it. Let us take the right message in the right way to those in need. May God bless you as you take an active part.

Chapter seventeen

Decision Making and the Will of God

PEOPLE SEEM TO THINK THERE is something deep and mysterious about finding God's will for our lives, as though the complexities of the universe are wrapped around the will of God, and we need to untangle it all in order to know what He has for our individual lives. Nothing could be farther from the truth. God never says, "I have a wonderful and blessed plan for your life, but I'm hiding it from you. Try and find out what it is." That is so far from the character and thinking of God.

The whole theme of the Bible is that God delights to be known. He knows you and wants you to know Him, and He enjoys leading His children into the abundant life He has planned for them. He wants you to find His will for your life, and He offers the knowledge of His will freely to all those who really want to know it. This is the foundational concept for considering decision making and the will of God, and it will always guide us in the right direction.

The Bible gives two basic descriptions of how to find the will of God. One is for beginners, as God wants His little ones to find their way easily. The other is for His older children, as they learn and grow and are ready to assume more responsibility. Both tell us that God is committed to leading His children.

There have been many entire books written about all the aspects of decision making and the will of God, and you may feel that it is rather presumptuous to think I can encapsulate the whole issue in two simple concepts. Books of experience in following the Lord are always helpful and will certainly be worth your time. However, for help with the simple, practical basics in finding the will of God for your life, these two concepts will open the door to an awesome, every day walk with the Lord which brings confidence in His leading for each step of the way.

God's will for beginners

This one is simple, as you may imagine, so even a child or a babe in Christ can do the will of God. It is outlined in Proverbs 3:5-6 and will enable even the newest believer to make good decisions. You will notice, however, that it allows young ones to do the will of God, although they may not know or understand the will of God at the outset.

These verses say very clearly that if you will put your life, including your decision making, completely and unreservedly into His hands, He will get you to the right place at the right time to do or say the right thing. "Trust in the Lord with all your heart" is absolute, continual surrender to His best for you. "Lean not on your own understanding" means not being molded by circumstances or peer pressure, the only basis for our understanding. "In all your ways acknowledge Him" means giving Him the option to do what He knows is best in each and every situation. "He shall direct your paths" is His promise to help you do His will, even when you don't understand it.

In other words, God, the gracious Father, is willing to take full responsibility for any child of His who will allow Him to do that. In practical terms it means simply meet each of those first three things freely from your heart, make your decision, and you cannot make a mistake. If need be He will simply carry you, physically, mentally or spiritually helping you make the right choices. You will be able to look back on it and see clearly that the right decision was made and carried out.

We see it all the time with a caring father making sure his young child does the right thing, even in situations the child cannot begin to understand. A good father does not attempt to explain everything to a little one, hoping the child will somehow do the right thing. Often the father simply picks up the child to get him into the right place or out of the wrong place, lovingly directing and guarding until the child can begin to understand for himself. This is God's way of leading His little ones who depend on Him completely, as outlined in Proverbs 3:5-6.

God's will for His older children

God expects something different from His older children, those who have more experience in their relationship with Him. Romans 12:1-2 give us the outline for this stage of finding God's will, and you will notice that it includes knowing His will, instead of merely doing His will. You will also notice that this stage requires more time, more thoughtfulness, and more effort, as befitting an older child who is ready for more responsibility.

It begins in the same place – complete and conscious daily surrender – which it refers to as being very reasonable. The next step involves clearing the deck, intentionally moving away from the world's decision making process, committing to conforming to God's way, rather than being pushed into the world's mold. Then comes transformation, the part which takes time. I call it God's replacement plan, detailed in Ephesians 4-5 and Colossians 3. As it is outlined here in Romans, it entails renewing your mind – getting rid of worldly thinking and replacing it with godly thinking found in the Bible. As what you are learning from God's Word gradually replaces what the world has impressed upon you, verse two says you will be able to understand the will of God.

The father/child analogy again helps us understand. As a child gets older, the tutelage of the father hopefully shapes his thinking to the point where the child begins to grasp the underlying concepts, as well as the simple directions. The child is then able to make choices based on those concepts and no longer needs the father's personal input at every turn. The best case scenario is that the child can face any situation and make good decisions because he now intimately knows what the father would do in that situation.

Thus it is in this second concept in knowing the will of God. As we see God's direction through the first concept, we develop a basic idea of where He is going and how He intends to get there. As we move away from the world's mold and allow the Word of God to shape our thinking, we begin to understand underlying ideas and know why God is doing things. The result of our faithful application of these two concepts allows us to reach the point where we will know what He would do in any situation, and we will make good choices because we have come to understand the will of God and have made it our own. We will begin to do the will of God instinctively, because we now know what He would do in that situation. The will of God ceases to be a mystery and instead becomes our way of life.

Dad's long-term plan for knowing Jesus, for having "the mind of Christ"

Starting in Matthew, go through the Gospels. Each day, read only until you find a verse that tells you something about Jesus. It may tell you something He said, something He did, His reaction to something or even what someone said about Him, anything that gives you insight into His way of thinking, being, acting or reacting. Then take a minute or two to memorize that verse, to store it in your mental data bank. The next day, review only the verse from the previous day before proceeding to the next verse to repeat the process.

One verse at a time, consistently, daily, will gradually build into your mind Jesus' way of thinking, the ultimate application of Romans 12:1-2. It doesn't take much time on a daily basis, but the cumulative effect is the key to transformation. I always felt that this kind of approach was putting things into my mind for the Holy Spirit to use as He would, giving Him something to work with when He needed it.

As far as I can remember from approximately thirty years ago, it took me about four years to work through the Gospels in this way, but it changed my life. I found myself thinking and responding in a manner similar to the way I had watched Jesus think and respond. It was much easier to make decisions with confidence. I was more peaceful and aware of what God was doing in the world around me, feeling like I could more easily fit into His plan. It was simpler to help others with their questions. The ramifications seemed endless, a blessing to me and to those to whom I ministered.

In something I heard or read since Jesse's home going, I got the impression that he had either completed this plan or was working on it. I would not be surprised, as he was that kind of man, especially when it came to knowing Jesus better. He and I recommend it to you for your growth and blessing, as well.

References: - seeking Jesus' thoughts: Matt.7:24-25, Phil.2:5, Isaiah 11:2, 1 Cor.1:24, Phil.3:7-12, Col.1:9, 1 Peter 4:1-2 - the transforming power of the Word: Ps.119:9&11, Romans 12:1-2, Eph.4:20-24, Col.3:10 - consistency important: John 8:31-32, Phil.3:13-14, Col.2:2-10, 3:13, 2 Tim.2:15, 3:14

The advantage of doing God's will

Yielding to temptation means exchanging a moment of pleasure for a lifetime of shame. Conversely, yielding to God's will means perhaps passing up on a moment of pleasure to reap the benefit of a lifetime of shame-free blessing.

Legacies

Due to the transient nature of life in this fallen world and the proper "pilgrim" perspective we should have, we should focus on faithfulness in our immediate task, rather than on a legacy. If we concentrate on trying to insure a legacy, we may lose touch with what God wants us to accomplish. If we give attention to completing the job God has given us to do, an enduring legacy will be the natural result. Two examples may be instructive.

John Wesley had a nation-transforming ministry, and others, following his example, had a major impact in frontier America. However, when the attention changed to that of building or maintaining his legacy, the Methodist denomination, the impact gradually died. Wesley would be hard pressed to recognize today the work he began so effectively in the power of God.

Jesse set out to serve the Lord in whatever little ways he could, seeking only to grow and to be faithful to the Lord. He thought that his efforts were fairly insignificant but always sought to do his best. He died at twenty-four, but we are still hearing about the lives he touched and will continue to influence for the Lord, an incredible legacy for such a young man.

So, do your part in God's plan today, however inconsequential it may seem. Leave the future to those whom God will raise up to carry on His work, not yours. God seems to follow that pattern, anyway. Legacies will come, as needed, within that framework.

Plans A, B, and C for life

Too many Christians are so busy with plans B and C that they have no time for plan A, which would take care of B and C, as well. To truly enjoy a fulfilling life we must get away from a focus on B and C and give ourselves to an active pursuit of plan A. Let's look at these plans and see why.

Plan B calls for seeking and enjoying God's blessings in each day and in each part of our lives. Sounds spiritual, and it sure sounds pleasant. But it also sounds extremely selfish.

Plan C calls for seeking and pursuing spiritual warfare. Again, this sounds very spiritual, not to mention dramatic and challenging, which contributes to a feeling of importance, which many people are seeking these days. However, this is not a major focus of the Bible. Jesus came to destroy the works of the devil (1 John 3:8), not to fight him. Paul mentions spiritual warfare occasionally, but spends most of his time addressing plan A.

Plan A calls for sharing your life with God (John 14:21-23, 17:3) and sharing His life with others (Colossians 3:8-17). This is the true path to life, joy and fulfillment. It also covers plans B and C, as you will constantly experience God's blessings in their proper perspective, and the devil will never get the upper hand in your life. As Jesus taught and demonstrated, unselfish and God-centered always works best. Try it.

Our job

We each have a job to do within the larger scheme of things and will be judged on how well we do it. We each must bear some of the burden resulting from the fall, as we all have sinned, and thus we must each bear some of the responsibility of working toward the solution.

As we do our part we also will share the satisfaction of accomplishment in the ultimate victory.

The central idea is for teamwork between God and man, God's plans and power implemented through man's action. To look at it in another way, Jesus and His ministry are the central theme or strategy of history, and He will accomplish His plan and ministry. We are all subplots in history, successful and significant as we interface properly with His plan and purpose.

Concerning the means, we are not here to win the victory by beating the world at its own game – deceit, use of force, etc., but rather to win the world by a higher strategy, overcoming evil with good, against which they have no defense. Gandhi had the right idea or at least was on the right track, though his understanding of the truth and of the power of the Gospel was lacking. Thus, in dependence upon God and His power and guided by His truth and His Spirit, we are to do the individual jobs He gives each of us and for which He gives us strength and abilities and provision. God puts together what we each can do in order to accomplish His plan. This gives meaning and significance to our lives and something to lay at His feet as offerings that mean something to Him.

Free will – freedom within the fence

The question is, if God is sovereign and in total control of the course of history, doesn't that take away our free will? How can we truly have a choice if an all-powerful God is in control? Doesn't that make us robots, pawns in His master plan? The concept of "freedom within the fence" helps me understand the answer to that question, and puts it in the proper perspective that includes both sovereignty and free will, with its accompanying responsibilities and consequences.

The "fence" is the boundary of God's eternal plan and purpose. As I have already mentioned, He will assuredly accomplish what He has set out to do. No event or person will ever prevent that from being done. In other words, no person, no matter how smart, how rich, or how powerful, can break through or break out of God's overall plan. They can only be a part of it, as Nebuchadnezzar, the most powerful king in history, found out, becoming an instrument in the hands of God.

However, within that "fence", we have the freedom to choose, no matter how wisely or how poorly, and those choices have consequences for us and for the larger world in which those choices are made. If we make poor choices, the consequences are hardship, heartache and struggles. If we make wise choices, the consequences are joy, fulfillment and blessing for ourselves and for those around us. We would be wise to constantly take into consideration God's principle that we will consistently reap what we sow. There is both blessing and sorrow in that principle, depending upon our choices.

Down through the years, in the exercise of their free will, people have tried to break out of the fence, and we should be instructed by their examples. Nebuchadnezzar thought he was above the power of the fence, ran headfirst into it, and found himself not only contained but educated by God's sovereignty. Paul had a different experience when he tried to break out. He found himself face to face with Jesus, the keeper of the fence, yielded to Him, was redeemed, and never tried to break out again, having freely joined into God's eternal plan. Good choice, with the associated blessings.

Jesus similarly encourages us to choose wisely, to become part of God's plan, with the accompanying grace and blessing. That's the smartest choice we will ever make, as yielding to Someone who is wiser, loving and powerful is the ultimate exercise of free will. Choose wisely.

Blockages

Get things right with God before you expect any guidance from Him (Ezekiel 20). The corollary to this idea is don't expect God to show you His will if you don't really want to do it.

The source of discontentment

I was recently re-reading the accounts of the Exodus and God's promises to His people as He was leading them toward and into the Promised Land, and it struck me that they were promised that which we all long for but then are never satisfied with. He basically promised them peace and prosperity, health and happiness, His constant care and fellowship and daily blessing. In other words, stick with Me, and you'll live happily ever after. Sounds good, doesn't it? And yet, over and over again, they wandered away seeking something else. Sound familiar? Why is it that living happily ever after was not enough? Why is it not enough for us?

And then I was meditating upon the Lord's Prayer, thinking about it from the perspective of God telling us what we can expect Him to do for us if we pray properly, since this is what the disciples had asked Jesus to teach them to do. Basically it comes out the same way, trust in Me, and I'll provide all you need to live happily ever after. Nothing amazing. Nothing thrilling. Just all you need to live happily ever after. And yet, over and over again, we seek and pray for something more, as though living happily ever after is not good enough.

God promises it in the Old Testament. Jesus reaffirms it in the New Testament. It sounds like that's His plan. For us to begin to understand the will of God, we need to keep this foundational principle in mind, that God's purpose and plan for us is to share life with Him, and He'll provide all we need to live happily ever after. When we move away from that, looking for something else, we move out of joy and into discontent.

"I surrender all" – Now what?

Down through the years, the hymn "I Surrender All" has expressed for many Christians the desire of their mind and heart. Of their mind, in that they know intellectually that surrender to the Father's perfect love and will is the rational thing to do. Of the heart, in that the heart's greatest desire is to reciprocate that love by fully loving in return; surrendering to the One Who gave all for them. For this reason, this song often brings tears to the eyes and feet to the aisles in a depth of response triggered by few others.

However, as with many emotional responses, the moment passes. The poignancy of the experience fades on the way home, and one is left with the lingering impression of deep desire without a means of accomplishing that desire. The response was genuine, but the way to apply that response in daily life is not easily understood, which too often results in a further fading of the experience until it becomes simply a shadow on the heart until it is repeated with a similar experience. At a certain point, that repetition leads to a measure of guilt about responding without changing, failing God in some way when He has so obviously reached out to us.

So, how do we turn genuine response into life-changing action? How do we truly "surrender all" in our daily lives in a way that pleases God and satisfies the desire of our mind and heart? What significant steps can we take to experience surrender, rather than simply singing about it in an emotional way?

The writers of Psalm 119 give us an excellent, practical outline for realistic daily "surrender-in-advance" in just eight all-encompassing verses (33-40). If you will make these principles your daily prayer and mindset you can begin enjoying a guilt-free surrendered lifestyle. Spend some time with this passage and make it your guide for the daily surrender which is the way to apply "I surrender all".

You begin by asking the Lord to teach you His way with the desire and purpose of doing it. Then ask for understanding; so you can see how to apply what He teaches you. Then ask Him to override your will if you're headed in the wrong direction, thinking about the wrong things or looking in the wrong places, because His will is actually your aspiration, even when the flesh is weak. (David seconds that motion in Psalm 139:23-24, and Paul says that for it to work, we need to have God work in us both to will and to do of His good pleasure – Philippians 2:13.) Ask Him to establish His Word in your heart, as that is your true desire. And live a life of daily hunger and thirst for His Word and for righteousness, which Jesus says will result in that desire being satisfied (Matt.5:6).

If you will follow this plan daily, which, by definition, is what it means to surrender all, you will begin to reap the benefits of a surrendered life. You will see your life transformed into His image. He will give you the desire of your heart, as you first expressed it in response to that wonderful old song. And you will begin to live "I surrender all", rather than merely singing about it. God bless you as you take this to heart.

One last thought

In my years of working with college students who were seeking the will of God for their lives, I occasionally ran into someone who wanted to know the will of God to see if they wanted to do it. This never seemed to work out all that well, and they always seemed to struggle. The reason, of course, is that God doesn't respond to that kind of approach.

God is quick to show His will to those who want to share their lives with Him and want nothing more than to walk in His way. He's not really into playing games, as life is a deadly serious proposition, and He seeks to seriously bless those who are serious with Him. I guess what I'm saying is that if you really want to know and do God's will, you will find it easily; as He is delighted to lead anyone into the abundant life He designed for us.

Chapter eighteen

Homiletics

IN THIS CHAPTER, JESSE WANTED me to address sermon preparation, delivery and teaching style. I will attempt to do this, although it's a bit difficult to verbalize that which has taken the Lord years to make an instinctive part of who I am. Since Jesse was already a good teacher/ preacher, I assume that he was simply trying to find some ways to perfect that which he was already good at.

I have been told that I am a good preacher. In fact, at Jesse's memorial service his room mate said, right in front of Jerry Falwell, that Jesse thought I was the best preacher he knew. Now, I certainly would not go that far, knowing there are lots of great preachers out there, including Jerry Falwell. However, if sharing from the heart the joys of God's Word and the joys of knowing Jesus makes a good preacher, then I can do that.

Sermon preparation

Although many people now find it hard to believe, I was a shy, retiring teenager who was as nervous about standing in front of people as anyone. It's only because I had something important to share and knew the Lord was ready to help this "earthen vessel" to do that that I even thought of standing in front of people to speak. I have found that anyone can do well with a subject that is close to their heart, as Jesus is to mine.

This brings up the most critical point in sermon preparation. You've got to have something to say which means something to you. The old timers called it "fire in the belly". You need to be so consumed by the Word of God and by an intimate relationship with Jesus that you are no longer able to *not* preach. A comprehensive background in the personal study of God's Word is absolutely essential for this.

Then there's the practice. The wall of my childhood bedroom has heard more good sermons than most churches. I would be reading my Bible there, find something I thought was interesting, and begin to preach quietly, explaining it to the wall. This gave me experience in organizing my thoughts and then hearing how they sounded out loud.

In college I got involved with a jail ministry, an experience I would recommend to any aspiring preacher. We would sing a little, and then each person in the ministry team would preach a mini sermon. There is nothing like learning to preach in front of an uninhibited audience which will give you instant, blunt feedback.

In church, you can preach any way you feel like it, and people will be polite, smile and nod. In jail, if you are not making sense, or are not connecting with your audience, they let you know about it. They pull their blankets over their heads. They yell at you. They flush the toilet. They talk loudly to each other, ignoring you. They beat on the wall or shake the bars.

You learn to pay attention to your audience and make adjustments if you're losing them. You learn to say interesting things in interesting ways. You learn to speak so as to communicate your message in an interesting way which can be understood by your listeners, which is the point of a sermon. A sermon is not just an assignment to be completed, part of your job description. It is God's way of conveying eternal truths to human hearts. Thus, it bears doing well – for Him and for them.

A softer place to practice is in a nursing home, a place where you're always welcome. You don't have to be amazing to speak there. They're just glad you showed up. And it gives you a warm audience with which to practice organizing your thoughts and hearing how they sound out loud. They will also give you feedback, although in different ways. You will be able to see if what you're saying is interesting. If you pay close attention, you will be able to see if they understand. You can learn a lot, while the fact that they're just glad you showed up will support your self-esteem.

That's the essential background preparation for good preaching. Now we look at the immediate preparation, getting ready for this week's sermon. This depends some on the person and how you function, but the basic idea is that you must get the main concepts of the sermon into your heart and mind, your very being, if you hope to have them touch anyone else's hearts. Early on, I made a commitment with myself that I would not preach an idea which I had not applied myself to know how it worked. This has been a good guide for me and has prevented simple term paper sermons which have no heart. I recommend this to you, as well.

There is a story about some ministers getting together and discussing how they went about preparing for their sermons, which is instructive for our discussion. The first one said he laid out at New Years the outline for his year in preaching. The second one said he did that semi-annually, while the third one did so monthly. The fifth one started each Monday and the sixth one said he worked best under pressure on Saturday night. The last one was strangely quiet through all the other talk but finally was forced to share his strategy. He said he planned a long hymn for right before the sermon.

I really don't recommend the last two approaches. You need some time to get your thoughts together in your own head and heart before you can share them clearly in a way which will help others. You need to know where you're going before you can take anyone else there. An old axiom which has helped me is to be able to simply state the point of your sermon in one sentence. However long if takes for you to arrive at that confidence in your sermon is how long you need to take to prepare.

Personally, I usually work through a series of sermons on a particular topic, often related to the season of the year. Then I get the basic idea and outline in my head on Monday or Tuesday, so I can meditate on it all through the week. This allows ideas to gel in my thinking as I study more or have different experiences in daily life. Nearer the end of the week I begin to preach it in my mind when I'm driving or mowing the lawn or during whatever gives me mental freedom to do so. This helps me organize my thoughts and allows me to hear how they sound in sermon form, to see if they make sense, if they are interesting, or if they are too long.

I have several important things I check at this stage. Am I saying what the Bible says, or is this just some cool idea I had? Do the illustrations really apply? If not, I discard them, no matter how interesting they are. Is this something I personally know about or apply in my own life, so I can speak from experience? If not, I readjust my approach or discard the stray parts of the message in order to get back into familiar territory. And I go to my editor-in-chief, "Lord, what do You want to say this week?" I'm not necessarily seeking a verbal response, but I have found that this question gives Him a better chance to lead me, and often I receive a key thought which helps with the message.

This whole process integrates the ideas in the sermon with my internal thoughts. In other words, the sermon becomes a part of me. Only as I am able to preach from the heart, my inner self, can I hope to reach the hearts of my hearers. Otherwise, I am merely delivering a term paper or a book report, and you know how boring those can be, no matter how important the topic.

I have included below the simple outline for decent preaching which I give to my prospective new preachers, so they can see the basic elements of a good sermon, although they will tailor them to fit their needs and personalities.

Some Secrets of Decent Preaching

Preparation: Seek God's direction on what you should preach. Asking the question, "Lord, what do You want me to preach about?" gives Him the opportunity to begin to direct you. Then choose a subject or a Bible passage which is dear to your heart, because only messages from the heart reach the hearts of others. Then study what the Bible says, letting it direct your thoughts, rather than trying to make it say what you want to say. Be prayerful throughout the process. To be prepared to preach, you should be able to state the main point of the message in one sentence. Then practice a couple of times to make sure the message sounds all right and flows well. Pray!

Basic outline: This is merely a simple framework to help you get organized. Make it your own, and use it to accomplish your purpose.

Introduction
Introduce the subject in a way which demonstrates its value and its connection with everyday life.

Main point A: State your first point clearly and simply
Give the scriptural reference
Give a simple explanation
Give an illustration from everyday life which people can relate to

Main point B: State your second point clearly and simply
Give the scriptural reference
Give a simple explanation
Give an illustration from everyday life which people
can relate to

Main point C: State your third point clearly and simply
Give the scriptural reference
Give a simple explanation
Give an illustration from everyday life which people
can relate to

Summary
Tie all your thoughts together and summarize the main point with its application in people's lives, and challenge them to act on it. Give them something specific they should do as a response to this message.

Reminder: We are but earthen vessels (2 Cor.4:7). As we do our part, God is faithful to provide the power to help us and to minister to our listeners.

Sermon delivery

When I first began to preach, I thought people should listen because I had something important to say. Jail ministry cured me of that, and then I heard that Abraham Lincoln said he liked a minister who preached as though he was fighting bees. And I began to understand a preacher's responsibility to engage his audience, to do his part in making the sermon interesting.

Now I use every delivery style I can think of, varying them so that neither I nor my audience gets into a rut. Object lessons are helpful. Good illustrations, especially in the form of stories, are essential. I used visual aids whenever possible, the more interesting (sometimes weird) the better. Alliteration helps sometimes, but gets boring if used too often. I sometimes wave my arms (Lincoln would have approved). I fluctuate my volume and tone. An occasional shout punctuates important points and keeps the audience awake. A whisper accomplishes the same thing. I've been known to walk around now and then. However, these things must happen naturally, must not be contrived.

In other words, I enjoy preaching, and when I do, people seem to enjoy listening. I allow humor to come through, as that is who I am, but I rarely tell jokes, since people tend to remember the joke and forget the point, which is the priority. I don't try to affect a style or to imitate someone else, but I will incorporate any good technique I see.

I pay attention to the audience and make adjustments according to their response. I go after them using all my skills to engage them. I focus on positive faces and mostly ignore frowners (unless they become the majority). I ignore single sleepers (there's one in every crowd), but I do my best to keep everybody awake and actively engaged. The best indicator of how I'm doing along those lines is when someone spontaneously answers aloud a question I ask in the course of the sermon.

I often ask the audience to help me, especially with math problems or important history facts. The more they participate the more they get out of it, which is always the reason for the exercise. And one key element in all this is knowing when to stop – sooner is always better than later. Say what you need to say and quit. Repetitive rambling only dilutes the value of the message.

The preacher's responsibility in delivery is to do his job to the best of his ability. To blame the audience for not listening is a cop out. Communicating the message is the priority and whatever you can or should do to accomplish that goal should be done, and done with enthusiasm. If it really doesn't matter to you, why should your audience care?

Teaching style

There are so many teaching styles which work well for their users that I do not advocate any particular one. I have tried several and have come to the conclusion that only the Spirit of God can do any serious, life-changing teaching. So, with the Lord's help, find a style you're comfortable with, develop it to the best of your ability, and you will see God use it to edify others.

My best attempts have often not accomplished my purpose, but God used them in different ways for His purpose, for which I am very thankful. I have done my best to stress what I thought was the most important point in a sermon and had someone thank me afterwards for something else in the message which really touched their heart, sometimes something I was pretty sure I didn't even say. I have learned to do my best and leave the results with Him.

One time I was preaching about the five P's of something or other, and in my totally uninhibited approach, I brought five peas and lined them up on the front of the pulpit at the start of the sermon as memory aids for the congregation. When I got to each point, I would say "and the next P is…" and eat one of the peas in the line before explaining the point. I had a good time. The congregation got a kick out of it. However, all they remembered was that I had eaten peas during the sermon. Even I don't remember what the points were – success as an interesting sermon, failure as a memory aid.

If you think you can actually plan what people are going to get out of your sermon, you are sadly mistaken and will be consistently disappointed. If you do your part to the best of your ability and allow God to determine what people get out of the sermon, you will be pleasantly surprised and consistently blessed. It's a team effort. Do your part, and God will do His, although often not in the way you expect, which is one of the things that makes preaching interesting.

In conclusion, preaching as a job results in quite boring sermons and not much in the way of life-changing outcomes. However, preaching which comes out of a life-changing relationship with Jesus and is based in the transforming power of the Word of God, which results in preaching because one must, leads to interesting sermons and to help for the listeners. May God bless all you young preachers out there who seek that goal.

Chapter nineteen

Ministry

DEFINITION: MINISTRY IS USING YOUR God-given gifts under His guidance to help others in their relationship with Him. There are many ministries and ministry formats, but unless they fit into this definition, they are not truly ministry as God intended, no matter how good or helpful they may be. Lots of people do lots of nice, helpful things very well with the best of intentions, but unless they are truly working with God in His plan and way, they miss the point of ministry and may actually wind up doing damage.

An interesting example of this is found in kind people's response to deer in winter here in the north country. In the middle of winter, when the snow is deep, and the deer are obviously having a difficult time, these kind people want to "minister" to them by putting out hay for them to eat, never imagining the harm they are causing. The deer, although they may be having a difficult time, have been making adjustments in their eating habits, shifting from grasses to cedar branches, and their stomachs are adjusting accordingly. The sudden change in forage is a shock to their system which usually does more harm than good and can even be fatal.

In a similar way, attempts at "ministry" may wind up being detrimental good intentions which do more good for the "minister" than for those they are trying to help. In order to prevent this, which any good-hearted person would certainly want to do, it is essential to understand ministry from God's perspective. Thus the definition, which calls us into an intimate relationship with God; so we can share in His ministry. This is the essence of true ministry.

I know ministers who cannot give testimony to the personal saving grace of Jesus for the simple reason that they have never experienced it. They cannot lead anyone into a life-changing relationship with Jesus, because they've never been there themselves. Their work falls under the definition of social work – kind actions by nice people that often help others or do good in the world. But it doesn't fall under the definition of ministry, as they do not have God's personal input or guidance to offer to anyone else, no matter how good their intentions are.

Conversely, a businessman could do what falls under the definition of ministry, and I knew such a man, because I worked for him in his radiator repair shop for two years. He used his business as a platform from which to use his God-given gifts to help others in their relationship with the Savior. Everything about his shop and everything about what he did had one purpose – to point people to a personal relationship with Jesus.

He had Bible verses everywhere in his shop; so you could not face in any direction without seeing one. Most were simply welcoming invitations concerning the love of God. Some were challenging verses designed to move you out of your rut and into an awareness of God's loving plan for your life. One was humorous with a challenge – he had chalked onto his barrel heater, "This is hot, but hell is hotter."

He began each day with a Bible reading and opening prayer in his office and invited everyone in the place, workers and customers, to come and share it. If they came in, he would include them in his prayer. If they decided not to come in, that was fine, but he still included them in his prayer. I'll never forget how he used to pray on his birthday that God would send someone his way that day that needed to find the Savior. Both birthdays I was there, God answered that prayer, and his birthday was extra special to him for it.

He did excellent work and was interesting to watch, and when people came over to watch, he would engage them in spiritual conversations as he worked. If they moved away from him and came to watch me, instead, I picked up where he left off and continued the conversation. We had learned that kind of teamwork when we shared together in prison ministry, and it stood us in good stead at the shop, as well. It was not uncommon for either of us to stop what we were doing to help a customer find the Lord, if there was a need, because that's what we were really there for.

So, ministry happens wherever one of God's children uses what God has given them to help others further along in their relationship with the Lord. It may be in church or at work or at home or in any casual conversation, but the result is the same, someone is drawn closer to God. Anything else, no matter how well-intentioned or helpful, is simply social work which may or may not help the kingdom of God. Remember the deer.

The right attitude

During one of the many discussions about which of them would be the greatest (the wrong attitude), the disciples were corrected by Jesus as He pointed out again that they were called to serve, citing His own example, "Even as the Son of Man came not to be ministered unto, but to minister, and to give His life a ransom for many" (the right attitude). And when He sent forth the twelve on their practice mission, He concluded His instructions by saying, "Freely you have received; freely give" (the right attitude). Paul picks up the thought in the first chapter of Romans by saying that he is a debtor, not to Jesus, which would be the obvious thought, but to those who had not yet heard the Gospel. In other words, he had freely received and owed it to others to freely give.

These three incidents encapsulate the right attitude for ministry. We are not in ministry because we are great and wonderful and need proper recognition. We are in ministry because Jesus had pity on us poor sinners, redeemed us and gave us something to share with others. Only with this attitude can we meet the conditions laid out in the definition of ministry, because it is only this attitude which allows God freedom to work through us.

Paul, a right attitude minister, shares a couple more thoughts with us which help us understand the right attitude for ministry. In the first one, he points out that anything we possess which makes us worthy of being in ministry is a gift from God. We cannot take credit for it and should not receive praise for it.

In the second thought, he calls attention to our human frailty, calling us "earthen vessels." He is untroubled by that, since he knows that if anything of value is accomplished through our ministry, it will have to be done by the power of God, Who can use any yielded earthen vessel. In fact, Paul appreciates the fact that God can use him, in spite of his weakness (the right attitude).

In these two thoughts, Paul completely shatters any hope we would have of pride in achievement in ministry. However, in pointing out our total dependence upon God, he encourages us to "glory in the cross" and enjoy sharing in God's awesome work. And, though we are extremely unworthy, except by the grace of God, we are invited to come alongside and share with God in His life-changing work, an amazing privilege which yields the right attitude for meaningful ministry.

Although I tend to be a little idealistic, I assume that, if you are reading this, you have a heart to understand how to do meaningful ministry. Therefore, you won't mind when I tell you that you must lay aside your pride and ambition and, in complete surrender to Jesus, the ultimate Minister, give yourself to first serve Him and then to serve those He calls you to. Only in this way can you hope to have a successful ministry in His eyes, which is the only recognition that is truly worthwhile anyway.

The right ministry

Another important aspect of ministry is to make sure you're in the right one. This is implied in the definition, that you're doing what God wants you to do, utilizing the gifts He has given you for that ministry. Much struggle and disappointment in ministry come when people try to do some ministry for which they are not suited. Paul lays this concept out for us in the twelfth chapter of Romans, the twelfth chapter of 1 Corinthians and the fourth chapter of Ephesians.

In these chapters, he explains that God has given people various gifts for various ministries in order to cover all the bases, and that each ministry is vital to the life of the church. Thus, it is important that we each do the ministry that God has given us to do to the best of our ability with His help. We should never envy the ministry of others or try to do something outside our gifts, just because that seems more important or gains more recognition. The struggle and disappointment comes along when we try to force some ministry outside of our gifts.

A personal example may help. From the moment I found Jesus I have wanted to share that joy with others, and evangelism seemed the ultimate ministry. I went to various seminars to learn methods, got involved in several evangelistic ministries and preached my heart out, all to find out that I did not have the gift of evangelism. So, rather than setting out to be the next Billy Graham (who definitely has the gift of evangelism), I followed the Lord into the ministry He had for me. In doing that I was better able to use the gifts God gave me and have been successful in that ministry. Ironically, proceeding along the Lord's path for my ministry has enabled me to lead scores of people to the Lord, fulfilling my initial desire, as well.

Therefore, to find success and fulfillment in ministry, follow the Lord's direction, utilizing His gifts, and don't envy or try to be someone else. Remember, ministry is first and foremost service to the Lord. If you follow Him in what He has for you and work with Him where He wants you, you will enjoy His care and blessing, and your ministry will be successful in His plan.

The right purpose

There are a variety of motives for doing anything, many of which do not apply well to ministry. Getting rich, getting famous, meeting girls, for example, are never good motives for ministry, although they have been used as reasons for entering ministry, because people can get off course in any endeavor, even in ministry. The motive which provides the right purpose for ministry is the desire to live in obedience to the Lord in order to help others in their relationship with Him.

Even this motive can get off track if we minister for what we can get out of it. We must focus on the obedience to the Lord part, serving Him first of all, which allows Him to use us in His plan to help those around us. If our purpose is to serve Him, we will be free from worry about receiving anything in return from the people we serve, which Jesus says can be a problem, because even sinners help others in order to get something in return. The freedom to minister to others without concern for what we can get is a wonderful freedom to share with the Lord in His work, which is ample reward in itself.

Therefore, the right purpose for ministry is to give, not in order to receive, but in order to share in the Lord's work of helping others, knowing that if we do this, the Lord Himself will look after us, giving us all that we need in return. There is great liberty in depending upon God for all of our emotional, spiritual and physical reward for ministry. This is the essence of a working relationship with Him – we work with and for Him, and He provides all we need to do that and blesses us with joy in ministry besides, independent of the response of the people we serve.

This concept also frees those we serve from any pressure to respond out of human guilt or expectation.

It gives them the liberty to respond to the Lord's ministry through us and to give their hearts to Him and what He is doing in their lives, without worrying about our reaction. In other words, if we will serve with the right purpose, it gives us freedom to minister properly, people freedom to respond properly, and the Lord freedom to do His thing unhindered by strange motives, expectations and reactions.

Let us purpose to give ourselves freely to the Lord and to others, as the Lord gives Himself freely to us. This allows us to share in His ministry and allows Him to accomplish His purpose in and through us. This is the true essence of ministry that matters, which impacts our lives, as well as the lives of those we serve, and blesses the world as God is able to use us.

Bonus feature

A Shepherd's Story

IT HAD BEEN A ROUGH *year, trying to cope with my grief. I had preached every Sunday, something only Jerry Falwell really understood when I told him. He called it "preaching through it", something he understood, because he had had to do that himself at times.*

And yet, at Christmas time, I wasn't sure I had anything left to preach which would uplift and encourage others. Grief had taken a lot out of me. I wasn't sure I could feel the spirit of Christmas this year. I guess, subconsciously, I wasn't sure God was thinking of this world-weary country boy laboring up in the hills.

As I pondered the first Christmas from that perspective, the following story came into my mind. As I wrote it down, even my subconscious began to understand again the warm love of God which reaches into the coldest places to encourage boys and girls who need strong arms around them to hold and protect them in difficult times. I began to see myself in that story and knew without a doubt that God was thinking of me just as He had been thinking of all the world-weary people back then.

God used this story to encourage and lift my heart. He gave me lots of good stuff to preach that Christmas to help others.

And now I share it with you, trusting that its warm love will reach your heart with the embrace of God Himself.

A Shepherd's Story
By Nathan Strong
December 2005

Roughly two thousand years ago, outside a little town called Bethlehem, there lived a ten-year-old boy named Micaiah. Though his friends called him Mike, his mother called him Mikey, as he was the youngest of too many children. His older sisters called him Mikey, too, though with a more sarcastic tone. His big brothers, who had no use for him unless there were chores to do, called him loser. His father, who had an alcohol problem, most often just called him "hey stupid", if he spoke to him at all. Theirs was not a particularly happy home.

They lived in a little run-down house with a little run-down barn out back. The house consisted of three small rooms. One was used as the living area, the kitchen, living room and dining room. This area was furnished with a small counter, a little table with two benches and a fire pit for cooking and for what little warmth it could provide. The table was too small to seat the whole family, so Mike always ate standing up, if he could work through the hungry crowd huddled close around the food.

As a result, Mike was small for his age. His mother called him wiry. His father called him scrawny. His brothers called him "little shrimp". His sisters occasionally felt sorry for him and slipped him a piece of bread when no one was looking.

The other two rooms were bedrooms, one for the parents and one for the kids. The kids' room had two beds, one for the girls and one for the boys. There was not enough room for Mike in the bed, so he had to make do with an old quilt, which he usually bunched up by the fire to sleep on, as it made him feel as though he had his own room.

Being at the bottom of the pecking order, Mike always got the worst jobs, the chores no one else wanted to do. If the barn needed cleaning and everyone else was "too tired", Mike got to do it. When they needed to move their stubborn old donkey, which had vicious hooves and knew how to use them, they sent Mike around in back of him with a stick to get him moving and to dodge the wild kicking. And when someone needed to go out with the sheep on a cold night, Mike had the privilege of that job, as well.

Mike didn't mind that chore so much, because it gave him an excuse to get out of that dreary house, and the other shepherds always treated him kindly, knowing a little of what he went through at home. They let him bring his little flock up beside theirs where they would be safe. They let him share the warmth of their fire, and, inevitably, some softhearted soul would give him something to eat. He loved the fresh air and the star-filled sky, and it took his mind off his troubles for a while.

Those troubles always came right back when he got home in the morning, though. However, Mike was too stubborn to get too discouraged. Just like their old donkey, he kept on, making the best of things.

As time went on, he became more and more convinced that no one really cared about him. His family didn't show any love that he could see or understand. They only went to synagogue halfheartedly when they had to, so he had no comprehension of a God who might have loved him. His greatest encouragement was the thought that sooner or later he was going to grow up and get out of there. He would have his own life, and no one would be ordering him around any more.

One late December night, as Mike was trying to get comfortable in his old quilt by the fire, he heard the familiar, slurred "hey stupid" and knew whose turn it was to go out with the sheep tonight. He wrapped his quilt around him like a poncho against the cold and went out to get the sheep moving to the nighttime grazing grounds. The other shepherds greeted him warmly, made a place for him by the fire, and one offered him some of his supper. Contented, Mike looked around at the star-filled sky, the moonlit hills, the quiet sheep scattered over their pastures, and settled in for a peaceful night. *This is my favorite spot in the whole world,* he thought, while the pleasant scene brought peace to his troubled heart, as it always did.

Mike was asleep with some of the others, as a few stood watch, when suddenly the sky was ablaze with a supernatural light, waking everyone up. As they blinked in the unaccustomed brightness, they heard a voice, a deep and wonderful voice that seemed to fill the heavens and reach to the depths of their hearts. Some were afraid, but Mike, used to being confronted with just about anything, was only amazed, searching for the source of that voice that seemed to be filled with a kindness that made him hungry for more.

When the authority of that voice filled the night sky, it seemed as though it was speaking directly to him, as Mike heard him say, "I bring you (me?) glad tidings of great joy, which shall be to all people. For unto you (me?) is born this day in the city of David a Saviour, which is Christ the Lord. And you (me?) shall find this babe…"

As the voice went on Mike was overwhelmed with a new and captivating thought that lifted his heart as nothing ever had before. There *was* a God, and He did care about this little shepherd boy. He had gone to a lot of trouble to share this wonderful news with him. As the night sky reverberated with the most wonderful music Mike had ever heard, he let it wash over him in what seemed like waves of the heretofore unknown goodness of God. What a glorious night!

When it stopped as suddenly as it began, it left Mike gasping for breath, as though his very lifeline had been cut. Around him, the others were rubbing their eyes and shaking their heads as though waking from a dream. Gradually, they all agreed that it wasn't a dream, and they decided to go find this baby the angel had told them about. Mike followed along as they left the hills in search of a manger.

As he stood there in awe beside that humble manger, Mike was enveloped by an extraordinary warm sensation, almost like being wrapped in a comfortable quilt by a cozy fire. Suddenly he realized what it was, something he had very seldom felt before. This little stable was filled with the warmth of love. He'd never experienced that in his own barn, with its ornery donkey kicking the walls. Sadly, he'd rarely even felt that in his own little house.

He closed his eyes. This was such a delicious feeling. He wished it would never go away, that he'd never have to go away. He hugged himself with the delight of it all, listening to the quiet animal noises, the murmur of adoring voices, the rustle of hay, the chortling of pigeons in the rafters. Tonight they all seemed to be the sounds of love, love that kept saying what the angel had said, that this was all for him.

As much as he wished against it, with his eyes tightly shut, it did have to finally come to an end. The baby was hungry. The animals had grown impatient for breakfast. The shepherds had to get back to their sheep. The innkeeper began to look like he wanted to collect money from the extra occupants of his stable.

With a final wistful look at the wondrous baby, Mike wrapped his old quilt tightly around him, as though he could keep the newly encountered warmth close to himself, and went out into the morning. The cold air brought him back to reality, like the coldness of his little life. As the other shepherds excitedly told everyone they met the wonderful news of what they had experienced, Mike trudged home with his head down, knowing that no one in his house would even care to hear about what he had seen that night. They couldn't take it out of his heart, though; this newfound hope and love that he was sure could carry him through anything, no matter how hard, no matter how long.

In spite of the odds to the contrary, Mike did grow up. He did get out of there. When he left home, however, he didn't just leave that house or even that town, for that matter. Taking advantage of his new freedom, he moved clear across the country, finally settling in the hills above the Sea of Galilee, good sheep country, which was ideal, as that was all he knew.

He worked hard. He knew how to do that. Through the years, he built up his own flock of sheep. He fixed up a little house and barn out in the hills. He married a local girl and started a family of his own, making sure that they received better care than he remembered. By the time he was forty, he could look around with pride at what he had accomplished. But, in reflective moments, especially out with the sheep at night, he would gaze up into the stars and wonder what had ever happened to that baby in the manger in that little, love-filled stable.

In those moments, when it all seemed like a dream, he would remember the warmth that had enfolded him, look around at how far it had brought him, and know without a doubt that it was true. He would turn his eyes to the brilliant, glittering stars and talk to God, the

One Who had showed him on that long ago night that He was there and that He loved him. He would talk to Him simply, always first thanking Him for the chance to see such a wondrous thing. He would thank Him for caring for a simple shepherd boy and for helping him all these years. And, as he prayed for his wife and his children, he would pray for that baby in the manger and wonder some more.

Mike was out with his sheep one afternoon when he saw a crowd come up the valley and spread across the hillside opposite him. He left the sheep with his helpers and crossed the valley to see what it could be. A young man was speaking kindly in a deep and wonderful voice which seemed familiar somehow, though Mike couldn't think why. The man spoke of the love of God as though he knew it well. As he listened, Mike was transported back to that night and that stable. Those treasured memories resurfaced, more vivid than ever, and he wondered what possible connection there could be.

In the days and months that followed, whenever that man wandered with his followers through the area, Mike went to listen some more. Such graciousness, kindness, wisdom and authority he had not heard or felt since that night, such as could only be from God Himself, Mike was sure. He watched him heal the sick. He heard that he had calmed a storm on the Sea of Galilee, one that had harried Mike's sheep until it had suddenly and mysteriously stopped. So many good, some would say miraculous, things he heard and saw. He soaked up the wonderful teaching and spirit that the young man shared, feeling again that it was being offered just to meet the needs of his heart, as though he had been waiting for this for years.

He also had a chance to question some of the crowd and found out that the young man was from Nazareth. This seemed to be a dead end in Mike's questioning, until someone told him that he had actually been born in Bethlehem, because of the Roman census some thirty years ago. At that bit of information, the spark of interest in his breast burst into a consuming flame. Now he knew he must talk with him.

The young man seemed kind and approachable, which helped overcome Mike's feelings of unworthiness. However, it was when the man welcomed some children that he felt like he might even welcome an old shepherd boy, and Mike joined the line to go talk with him. Even so, he was totally unprepared for the response he got when he reached the front of the line and shyly extended his hand to say hello.

The young man embraced him and exclaimed, "Mike, it's so good to see you. It's been a long time since that night in the stable, hasn't it? You've grown into a fine man, and with a family of your own. What a blessing to have you here!"

In that instant, Mike heard the soft sounds of a quiet barn. He smelled the fresh hay and the warm animals nearby. The wonderful warmth of that night in the stable flooded back over him, as though he was wrapped in that old quilt again, feeling that heavenly love again for the first time. It did not seem strange at all that this young man knew his name, knew all about him, cared for him as no one else ever had. Mike felt like he did on that long ago night, and it felt marvelous. It felt like he had come home, home where he belonged.

This time, he couldn't wait to get home to tell his family.

Appendix

New Normal

I̅N̅ ̅T̅H̅E̅ ̅F̅I̅R̅S̅T̅ ̅F̅E̅W̅ ̅M̅O̅N̅T̅H̅S̅ *of our grief after Jesse died, I went through the regular struggles with grief which any father faces, struggles which seemed overwhelming at times. Only my faith kept me sane. However, as I am used to dealing with things in writing, one day I sat down to record my struggle. The result felt like a therapeutic gift from God, especially since the day on which it all poured out was my birthday.*

As it helped me, I printed it out to share with others who faced similar situations. I originally intended to share it with Jesse's unit, which is why it has the heading it does. However, when they said it helped them cope, and others have said the same since, I have included it here. You will understand a little of what I have been through, and perhaps it will help you.

NEW NORMAL

Thoughts from Sgt Strong's Dad

With Jesse, our Marine son, in Iraq, we knew precisely what it meant when two Marines in dress blues came to our door. Somehow, we survived hearing them tell us that our son had been killed in action. God graciously held us in His arms as we dealt with the initial shock, called our other two children to tell them the news, and endured our first night of grief.

Thus began the process that would forever change the way we dealt with life. We rode the emotional rollercoaster that was the media onslaught, the comfort of friends, the memorial service, the paper work, and our bodies' physical responses, while trying to keep up with the everyday things of bills, jobs and housework. It was an emotional jumble of blessings and sorrows that made each new day a new challenge. We are still learning to cope.

Following a traumatic occurrence such as this, it is intuitively obvious to those involved that nothing will ever be the same again, that there will forever be a new normal. We have to realize that things won't ever be as though nothing has happened. People around us also have to decipher how to relate to our situation, wanting to help without hurting. The result is confusion and unexpected stress, both internally and in our relationships.

Things that seemed very important before are now insignificant. Things that seemed trivial before, take on new, often overwhelming, significance, which may or may not be understood by those around us. For example, when someone around me speaks of thinking they should spend more time with their children, I have a passionate response that I have to fight to control. I want to shout, "Do it now!"

Everywhere I go, everywhere I look, I see things that move me, reminding me of my son. They are all good memories, as that is the way he was, but they also remind me of my loss, and that's tough on my heart. I'll never escape them, don't want to, but I have to figure out how to process them properly.

The problem is that you are moving into unknown territory for which you have no training or experience. And most of the people who offer advice have no training or experience either. They always have good intentions, but can only tell you what they think they would do in that situation. So you are on your own, and the resulting actions and reactions aren't weird, but new normal, to be evaluated and revised as time goes on, but not to be feared or to be worried about.

Last week they brought us our son's things from Iraq. Now what do we do with different reactions to each item? It felt nice to have things of his, but hard to have them remind us of our loss. His watch seemed particularly comforting, as he was wearing it that night.

Then the alarm went off at 11 pm Iraqi time, the time he awoke for his appointment with destiny. Welcome to new normal.

So if I wear my son's lapel chevrons and people mistakenly assume that I'm doing that to keep him near or to give me chances to talk about him, that's okay. I actually wear them because it steadies me somehow, and that's not wrong. It's new normal, and I have no idea why it does that or how long it will do that. It just helps for now, whether others understand or not.

New normal includes a variety of new experiences. There are the unexpected tears at inopportune times. There is forgetfulness that leaves you wandering in a daze. At times you can't decide what to have, as the waiter stands at your table. And that's just the start.

Not to worry. People will wait while you dry your tears. Post-it notes can keep you on track. Waiters are paid to be polite in any situation. You find yourself in a period of grace while you're finding new normal.

Then there's the traumatic occurrence itself. People tend to tip-toe around it, unsure of what to say or what to do. It's a learning time for everybody involved. We found it helped to talk about things, especially with people who were understanding. Those who were patient and willing to talk about our son and his death helped us learn to cope.

Your relationship with the world has also changed. New patterns of fitting in have to be learned, and people have to figure out how to relate to you in your new setting, as well. Others have to keep on with their lives while you are still trying to deal with your trauma. It's like dropping out of a hiking party to explore, and look up to find the group has moved on , and you now have to catch up to rejoin them. Except, in this situation, it is kind of hard to yell, "Wait up!"

Another factor in new normal is the establishment of a new identity. For years to come I will be viewed by others as the father of the Marine who died tragically in Iraq. I don't feel like a different person than I was before, but it's as though I've been set aside as a monument to my son for others to salute as they go by. As the world goes on around me, I'm trying to discover how I can rejoin the human race, sort of like getting on a moving merry-go-round.

Thankfully, Jesus is the constant, the solid rock, of my new normal. Jesus, who died for me. Jesus, who said, "I will not leave you comfortless. I will come to you." Jesus, who promised, "I will never leave you or forsake you." What an anchor He has been.

When, as a teenager, I gave my life to Jesus, He also gave His life to me, to be all that I will ever need. No day is too hard for Him, no matter how difficult it is for me. No puzzle is too confusing for Him, no matter how confused I am. He will always be there, walking each step of the way with me, ready to listen to the cry of my heart. His Word instructs me and settles my thoughts. His Spirit guides me, comforts and teaches me. His power gives me calm assurance that I will find new normal and will be able to function successfully again.

Below are some Scripture passages that have helped me along the road toward new normal. I share them with the hope that they will encourage you, too.

This verse is the awesome foundation of the living hope I have:

"Blessed be the God and Father of our Lord Jesus Christ, which according to His abundant mercy has begotten us again unto a living hope by the resurrection of Jesus Christ from the dead."
- 1 Peter 1:3

These verses not only comfort me but help me with understanding some of the purpose of my heartache:

"Blessed be God, even the Father of our Lord Jesus Christ, the Father of mercies, and the God of all comfort;
Who comforts us in all our tribulation, that we may be able to comfort them which are in any

trouble, by the comfort wherewith we ourselves are comforted by God."
- 2 Corinthians 1:3-4

This old, familiar verse comforts and helps me, because it reminds me that He is the perfect Guide, having been through the valley Himself:

"Yea, though I walk through the valley of the shadow of death, I will fear no evil: for Thou art with me; Thy rod and Thy staff they comfort me."
-Psalm 23:4

So, that's what I've been thinking about, trying to cope with a different world, working toward new normal. If you'd like to talk about Jesse, Jesus or about a traumatic occurrence of your own, please feel free to contact us. We'd be glad to talk with you. God bless you.

Nathan & Vicki Strong
1367 Creek Road
Irasburg, VT 05845

(802) 754-2790

marinemom80@mailstation.com   www.jessestrong.com

12864214R00136

Made in the USA
Lexington, KY
03 January 2012